IN
SEARCH
OF
BALANCE

IN SEARCH OF BALANCE

Virginia R. Mollenkott

WORD BOOKS, Publisher

Waco, Texas   London, England

Just behavior is a mean between doing injustice and
suffering it.

—Aristotle, *Nichomachean Ethics*, V. v.

There are then a great number of truths, both of faith
and morality, which seem contradictory, and which all
hold good together in a wonderful system. The source
of all heresies is the exclusion of some of these truths;
and the source of all the objections which the heretics
make against us is the ignorance of some of our truths.
And it generally happens that, unable to conceive the
connection of two opposite truths, and believing that
the admission of one involves the exclusion of the other,
they adhere to the one, exclude the other, and think of
us as opposed to them. Now exclusion is the cause of
their heresy; and ignorance that we hold the other truth
causes their objections.

—Pascal, *Pensees*, XIV. 861.

Paradox reveals and reinforces very simple truths—perhaps, really, only one simple truth, that Truth is One.
It does not *argue* that this is so . . . it demonstrates that
fact by its own operation, circling and spiraling about
its central fixed point, always deepening, thickening,
reinforcing our awareness of how multiplex any simple
truth is.

—Rosalie L. Colie, *Paradoxia Epidemica*, p. 519.

For Libra

CONTENTS

One

When I turn to [the Bible] . . . , what I find is helpful . . . but not without its problems. I do not find a list of rules which I am able to follow explicitly so that I am exempted from the nitty-gritty of choice.

Chapter One:

CHAOS AND COSMOS

I have lost my balance—that is, if I ever really had any. I guess the fact is that I never really had any. It was not very many years ago that this awful realization hit me. I had lived without balance because I had not really known who I was. Actually, I had not even known what I liked or didn't like.

Don't misunderstand me. I had achieved a Ph.D., and on the surface I looked anything but indecisive. My lack of balance stemmed from a tacitly assumed concept of God which had turned me into a drifter.

One day a friend put his hands on my shoulders and shook me. "If you don't like your circumstances, *do* something about them! You are not a victim!"

You are not a victim. Driving home that afternoon, I thought about those words. *You are not a victim.* I had never before realized that my concept of God and therefore of life had cast me in the role of a victim who had only to adjust to whatever happened, most of which was beyond my control.

In Search of Balance

It had never occurred to me that by the way I programmed my thinking, I was largely responsible for the success or failure of my own ventures. Up to that point my successes had been largely God's mercy and the sheer determination to earn my place in the sun; my many failures were inevitable with the unrecognized assumption that I was only a tool, only an instrument, only a passive receiver of my fate.

Many a time I had discussed with sophomore literature classes a poem by T. S. Eliot about hollow men who are also stuffed men—hollow of meaning, that is, but stuffed with the straw of trivia. These men have "quiet and meaningless" voices, "paralyzed force," and shifty eyes. Because they cannot bring their ideas to reality, their impulses to action, they childishly play "Here we go round the prickly pear" until finally their world ends "Not with a bang but a whimper." They try to say "For thine is the kingdom"—they try to enunciate words which (if they were heartfelt) would bring purpose into their lives—but always the fearful Shadow falls "between the desire and the spasm" and chokes off their utterance.[1]

As I had discussed this poem with one class after another, it had never occurred to me that there was any sense in which a decisive and hard-working professor like myself might also be a drifter, a hollow person playing my own version of "Here we go round the prickly pear." It had never occurred to me for the simple reason that my view of God, of life, and of myself precluded such a thought. God was all-powerful; I was His creature; my whole purpose for being alive was to perform His will. I would know His will by the circumstances of my life . . . therefore, of course, my only liberty lay in adjusting to whatever the circumstances happened to be. To attempt a radical *change* of circum-

stances—to transfer to a different high school, for instance—
wouldn't that be running away from the will of God? I had
to stick out any unpleasant circumstances in which I found
myself; I had to adjust myself to whatever came down the
pike, snatching from the moments whatever pleasure I could.
And because I was basically optimistic and joyful, life was
never wholly wretched.

But in the quiet interim after the hurly-burly of graduate
work, it was a shock to realize that I needed to find a reasonable balance in my concept of God and life and myself,
something I could build on, something I could live with. It
was a shock to realize that I had been heading toward the
fate Eliot describes in "Gerontion": becoming "an old man
in a dry month," or a "dull head among windy spaces." [2] It
was a shock to realize that even *I* could become an aged person such as Yeats describes, "a tattered coat upon a stick," a
scarecrow. I had seen a few scarecrows in my time—old
people who sat and stared at TV all day because their minds
were devoid of any thoughts worth thinking. Their souls
had never learned how to sing. But I had always assumed
that my education had made it impossible for me ever to
become a scarecrow. It was a shock for me to realize that my
soul, which like theirs was "fastened to a dying animal," [3]
would profit nothing from my education until that education
was organized around a hub which held practical meaning
for the way I lived.

Like many brought up in the evangelical tradition, I had
assumed that Christ was that organizing hub and that no
further thinking was necessary. But lately I began to wonder
whether Christ ever intended man to be as passive as I had
been; had He wanted His followers to be the mere victims
of fate?

I had read—I had even taught—words from Thomas

[15

Carlyle that never failed to move me. But at that crisis in my life, they excited me as never before:

> Here, in this poor, miserable, despicable Actual, wherein thou even now standest, here or nowhere is thy Ideal: work it out therefrom; and working, believe, live, be free. Fool! the Ideal is in thyself; the impediment too is in thyself: thy Condition is but the stuff thou art to shape that same Ideal out of. . . . O Thou that pinest in the imprisonment of the Actual, and criest bitterly to the gods for a kingdom wherein to rule and create, know this of a truth: the thing thou seekest is already with thee, 'here or nowhere,' couldst thou only see. . . . Be no longer a Chaos, but a World, or even a Worldkin. Produce! Produce! Were it but the pitifullest infinitesimal fraction of a Product, produce it, in God's name! 'Tis the utmost thou hast in thee: out with it, then. Up, up! Whatsoever thy hand findeth to do, do it with thy whole might. Work while it is called Today; for the Night cometh, wherein no man can work.[4]

Carlyle's existentialist doctrine of work, I labeled that passage for my students. And always I had felt that I was working up to my capacity. But suddenly Carlyle's emphasis on *order* struck me with great conviction. I longed to turn my life from chaos into cosmos, into an orderly world. But *ordered upon what principle?* I felt stumped exactly at the crucial point: "Whatsoever thy hand findeth to do." My hand found (and still finds) all sorts of things to do that other people didn't approve of; should I nevertheless do them with all my might? I knew then and know now that I can't live my whole life trying to please other people; but on what basis do I decide when to go my own way? or which way really *is* my own?

From discussion with students, colleagues, and friends I knew that other people experienced these conflicts, too. And the more I have thought about my own conflicts, the more I have seen that the *real* people around me (as opposed to the hollow men) are also embroiled in such conflicts. Recently in a newspaper I ran across two sonnets, each written by a different Columbia University professor, praising diametrically opposite ways of life. One argues for the dare-all, agony-ecstasy brand of living:

> They do not live who choose the middle way,
> Whom ecstasy and anguish have not known,
> Who scale no trembling heights, nor plumb the long
> Depths of an aching darkness in bright day.

The other one urges a conservative way of life:

> Blest they who see the stars yet walk the earth.
> In anguish keep the torch of hope aglow,
> Share equally life's sorrow and life's mirth,
> Hold beauty chaste and yet love's raptures know,
> Soul one with body, neither cloud nor clay.
> They only live who choose the middle way.[5]

So there you are: two perfectly intelligent men advocating opposites. And the trouble with me was (and continues to be) that I could see some truth in both of them—or perhaps that I lived like the first but admired the second. *Is it all a matter of temperament?* I wondered. But surely, by finding a firm footing, one could escape *some* of the veering vacillation which seems so wasteful.

As I have mentioned, I was brought up an evangelical Christian. That means I have been taught that the Bible is the only rule for faith and practice. But like most people of the twentieth century, from my wider environment I have heard something else again: that no authority can be trusted, that all values are subjective, that nothing is good or bad unless I happen to think it is. And it was right there that I found myself stuck every time: on what basis *do* I think an action is good or bad? Do I even *know* what I think?

George Bernard Shaw created a character named Tanner who draws a distinction between a child-mind and a true adult. The major distinction is the development of a personal and deeply believed moral passion:

> Our moral sense . . . is . . . a passion. . . . If it were not a passion—if it were not the mightiest of the passions, all the other passions would sweep it away like a leaf before a hurricane. It is the birth of that passion that turns a child into a man.[6]

Thinking that over, I realized that while I had always possessed a vaguely defined moral passion (defined mostly by the likes and dislikes of others as based on their very sincere interpretation of Scripture), I was also aware that men's "moral passions" can lead them astray—as witness the Inquisition and Fascist and Communist atrocities, and tragic incidents on both sides of the Civil Rights movement. It is possible to "do right" with a burning zeal and be wrong the whole time.

As a matter of fact, I have in my short lifetime observed only too many people who were demagogues within their own sphere of influence, burning with a "moral" zeal, absolutely assured that their will and the will of God were synonymous. If anyone criticized them, he was obviously of the Devil. Any attack was a Satanic attack. These people were totally off balance because it never occurred to them to question the rightness of their own thinking. They bulldozed other people in the name of Christ and apparently fell asleep without a minute's soul-searching. Within all religions, I suppose, their name is legion. But were they so different in their more noticeable way from what I was in mine? Pondering my own lack of balance because of overly negative self-concepts, and their lack of balance because of overly positive self-concepts, I have come to this conclusion: *the people who are most off balance are the people who never for a minute wonder about their own balance or lack of it.* They do not feel responsible to weigh alternatives because they are not really *aware* of alternatives. *No matter how decisively a person moves, he is a hollow man unless his life is self-examined and motivated out of a profound self-awareness.*

Throughout my continuing stages of self-examination (which will be a life-long process), another image out of T. S. Eliot has haunted me. In "Little Gidding," the final "gift" reserved for old age is "the rending pain of re-enactment" of everything that a person has ever done and been; the shame of discovering motives which until then have been hidden from himself; and the final realization that some actions were "ill done and done to others' harm" which at one time he had congratulated himself about, considering them virtuous deeds.[7] The possibility that what I currently think is virtue will some day be revealed to me as "ill done and done to others' harm" is horrible. I would like to avoid such a reenactment, to build fences against that eventuality. I suppose, however, it can't be helped. But still, I want as much light as I can get before I begin to bumble through.

Where to find that light? The Bible? I have been taught that the only rule for faith and practice is the Bible. When I turn to its pages, what I find is helpful, certainly, but not without its problems. I do not find a list of rules which I am able to follow explicitly so that I am exempted from the nitty-gritty of choice. Or rather, in the Old Testament I *do* find some rules which I immediately perceive I cannot keep in any absolute sense. (Under normal circumstances I can avoid murder, but I cannot avoid the flash of a hateful thought. And it is only miserable self-deception for me to deny that the hateful thought is the psychological equivalent of murder.)

But I have also been taught that my inevitable failures I can bring to Christ for redemption. The Bible assures me that the purpose of the law I cannot keep is precisely to show me my failure, so that I will turn to Christ. So far, so good. But what I now need is practical guidance for my present and future actions. Although I fervently believe in the redemption, it would be disgraceful for me to use the redemption as an excuse from living as decently as it is possible for me to live. So except for the important fact that I need not fear to face my failures and confess them to my Judge-Redeemer, I am confronted with the same practical problems as any other person.

What I find in the Bible is confusing in the extreme. I am supposed to have "simple faith" in what it tells me; but what *does* it tell me about the way I should live? That I must avoid even the appearance of evil—but that I must stand fast in the liberty of Christ; that I must pray without ceasing—but that I really do not know how to pray properly; that I must die to myself—but that I should live abundantly; that I should be subject to the powers that be in this world —but that I should obey God rather than man; that whosoever desires to come to God may come freely—but that in actuality no man can come to God unless God Himself draws him; that in society I must bear my own burdens—but that I am supposed to bear the burdens of others; that my righteousness is filthy rags in God's sight—but that He will bless me if I am persecuted for righteousness' sake; that I am to *study* the will of God—but that I am not supposed to lean on my own understanding; that according to Jesus everyone that is not against Him is for Him—but at the same time, everyone that is not with Christ is against Him; and on, and on, and on.

Just take that last contradiction. There is an enormous difference in those two statements. They form a paradox which can be rending, which *has* been rending (as I have personally experienced in churches which have stressed the one without the other). "He that is not against us is on our part" (Mark 9:40)—that statement stresses the total inclusiveness of Christ's love. The churches that emphasize it tend to blur all distinctions between the beliefs' of men, moving toward a rather bland sameness. (Why must we deny our distinctions in order to be loving?) On the other hand, "He that is not with me is against me" (Matt. 12:30). The churches which stress only *that* statement emphasize the exclusiveness of Christ, the demanding narrowness of a Christian commitment. These churches soon slip into fanaticism and a form of self-righteous slavery. (Why must we judge all those who don't see things precisely our way?)

Yet Christ made both statements, so both of them must be true. Or are they? Could it be that neither is true in isolation, except in its very special context,[8] and that their general truth depends on their being taught *together*? Is it possible that these opposites are *meant* to be kept in a meaningful tension with each other? Yet this is rarely done when men interpret the Bible for themselves or for others. Perhaps this is the cause of much of my confusion.

Paradoxes. Polarities of truth. Absurd contradictions, both of them somehow true at the same time. The Bible is full of them—but then, so is life. A psychoanalyst named Milton Sapirstein has written a book entitled *Paradoxes in Everyday Life*. Some of the paradoxes he gives are fascinating: that there is no better way to destroy a marriage than to present the newlyweds with a marriage manual; that a surprising percentage of neurotic children come from "happy" homes; that screaming mothers often have better-adjusted children than do unusually self-controlled mothers; that a person becomes enslaved to himself if he seeks the illusion of absolute freedom, refusing to make and abide by limiting decisions. "Men and women have begun to recognize," claims Dr. Sapirstein, "that sexual freedom is not the answer to their emotional problems. The false values of the last twenty or thirty years are becoming less prevalent; sober second thought is taking the glamor out of infidelity." [9]

But wait: what that twentieth-century psychoanalyst calls the paradox of freedom is an insight which has been available in the New Testament for many hundreds of years. One gains freedom only through meaningful voluntary limitation. It's paradoxical. It's self-contradictory. In a way it's absurd. But it's true.

Perhaps this is what I need to explore. Perhaps the balance I need lies in acceptance of the polarities of truth.

Perhaps.

References for Chapter One

[1] T. S. Eliot, "The Hollow Men," *T. S. Eliot: The Complete Poems and Plays, 1909-1950* (New York: Harcourt, Brace, & World, 1958), pp. 56-59.

[2] T. S. Eliot, "Gerontion," *T. S. Eliot: The Complete Poems and Plays, 1909-1950*, pp. 21-23.

[3] William Butler Yeats, "Sailing to Byzantium," *The Collected Poems of W. B. Yeats: Definitive edition, with the Author's Final Revisions* (New York: The Macmillan Company, 1956), p. 191.

[4] Thomas Carlyle, *Sartor Resartus*, ed. Charles Frederick Harrold (New York: Odyssey Press, 1937), pp. 196-197.

[5] Both sonnets were written in the 1930's. The first, by Irwin Edman, was published in the *Atlantic Monthly;* the second, by his friend J. E. Woodbridge, was previously unpublished. "Queries and Answers," New York *Times Book Review,* 1968.

[6] G. B. Shaw, *Man and Superman,* in *Major British Writers,* ed. G. B. Harrison (New York: Harcourt, Brace, & World, 1959), p. 725.

[7] T. S. Eliot, "Little Gidding," *T. S. Eliot: The Complete Poems and Plays, 1909-1950*, p. 142.

[8] Actually, in context both of Christ's statements support a single underlying principle, that a man's true allegiance is revealed by his actions. In Mark 9:40, John was upset that a man was casting out devils in Christ's name, and Christ said he should not be forbidden to do so because "he that is not against us is on our part." In Matthew 12:30, the Pharisees had accused Jesus of casting out devils by Beelzebub, the prince of the devils, and Christ pointed out that Satan could not cast out Satan without destroying his own kingdom. Therefore He ominously warned the Pharisees that "he that is not with me is against me." But none of this changes the fact that in different situations Christ emphasized different poles of truth, which have subsequently been perverted by being taught in isolation rather than in juxtaposition with each other.

[9] Milton Sapirstein, *Paradoxes of Everyday Life* (Greenwich, Conn.: Fawcett Publications, 1955), p. 172. For ample fictional

illustration of Sapirstein's point of view, read John Updike's *Couples* (New York: Alfred A. Knopf, 1968; Fawcett Paperback, 1969).

 Two

. . . when I seek to trust the Lord with all my heart,
and not lean on my own understanding, I must not
repudiate my own insights, nor must I refuse to
make responsible decisions.

Chapter Two

GOD'S POWER AND MY EFFORT

One of the biggest conflicts of my thinking has been over whether a person is rightly supposed to live for God, for others, or for himself. All my life I have been told that the formula for *JOY* was "*J*esus first, *O*thers second, *Y*ourself last." But when you think about it, that formula can get pretty contradictory and confused—as confused as the prayers of people who regularly offer thanks to God for their food but who never think of offering thanks to the human beings who earned and/or prepared the meal. If it is good to offer gratitude to God, why isn't it just as good to offer gratitude to His creatures? And doesn't neglect of the human dimension undermine the reality of the spiritual one?

By the same token, in what sense can a person divide living for *J*esus from living for *O*thers? And does living for *O*thers mean sacrificing my plans to theirs, my desires to theirs, my whole identity to theirs? Isn't that just about the most direct route to a whopping neurosis?

In Search of Balance

Tied in with these questions is the whole matter of human pride. I'm not talking about vanity; it is certain that the most revealing test of a man's spiritual size is what amount of glory it takes to go to his head. Some men are inflated by being elected treasurer of the local Parent-Teachers' Association; others remain unassuming after they have won the Nobel Prize. But those Nobel Prize winners, even those with the greatest spiritual capacity and consequently the most genuine humility—are they supposed to deny their own abilities and refuse to recognize their own greatness? Is it only the sin in me which makes my stomach turn when someone repudiates a sincere compliment with "It was all of God, sister; give Him all the glory"?

If a man practices eight or ten hours a day to become a great violinist, in what sense is it "all of God"? Or if another individual practices tremendous emotional control to curb his wild temper and succeeds in registering remarkable personal growth, in what sense is his growth "all of God"?

For that matter, I remember a case in my own life, a time when I had made a modest academic achievement. An atheist friend congratulated me, and suddenly I was seized with the desire to say the right thing. All my religious upbringing flooded my mind, and I answered with the voice of my childhood training rather than with the voice of my adult self, muttering that God had done it for me. My friend was shocked: "For goodness sake, Virginia, don't stand there and *deny what you have done!*" I wanted to run after her, somehow to explain that it was paradoxically possible for *me* to have done it while *God* did it through me; but I wasn't that clear on the subject. I have always remembered that encounter with a sense of shame and frustration.

The whole conflict came back to me recently as I listened to a wedding ceremony. The preacher assured the assemblage

that the bride and groom were being married not just because they loved each other, although that was important,
but primarily because *God* had brought them together. It
was *His* will that they be married, and they would say "I
do" because they were concurring with that will. I couldn't
help wondering what that emphasis would mean during a
family argument. Would they ponder darkly about why God
had done this nasty thing to them, bringing them together
when after all they didn't see eye to eye? Would they excuse
their own inadequacies with "This woman that *You* gave
me" or "This man that *You* gave me," as Adam did in the
Garden of Eden?

And I couldn't help remembering the very different emphasis in the wedding sermon which Dietrich Bonhoeffer
wrote in his Nazi prison cell:

> Every wedding is an occasion of joy, joy that human beings
> can do such great things, that they have been granted the
> freedom and the power to take the rudder of their lives into
> their own hands. The children of earth are rightly proud
> when they are allowed a hand in shaping their own destinies.
> And it is right that a bride and bridegroom should have this
> pride on their wedding day. It would be wrong to speak too
> lightly and irresponsibly about God's will and providence.
> To begin with there can be no question that it is your own
> very human wills which are at work here, which are celebrat-
> ing their triumph. The course you are embarking upon is one
> you have chosen for yourselves. . . . And so you alone must
> bear the responsibility for what you are doing, it cannot be
> taken from you. It is you, the bride and bridegroom, who as
> a married couple must bear the whole responsibility for the
> success of your married life, with all the happiness it will
> bring. Unless you can boldly say today: "This is *our* resolve,
> *our* love, *our* way," you are taking refuge in false piety. "Iron
> and steel may pass away, but *our* love shall abide forever." [1]

Provided that the bride and groom had been counseled that way and were not hearing all this for the first time, think what this emphasis would mean during family difficulties! Not an inch of elbow room for passing the buck! Only an awareness that making this relationship work is *my* responsibility because it was *my* free choice and determination in the first place. And such teaching would certainly cause people to think more carefully about their choice of life-partners. No room for "trial runs." No passive drifting into a marriage for lack of something better to do. Above all, no resigned acceptance of a partner because he seems to be the will of God for my life.

Yet surely there is a sense in which God *does* bring together two people who freely choose each other as life-partners. Right there lies the mystery to be explored. And there's no time like the present. Later for the related question of my own will versus the will of other people, including that of the church and society; now for the even more basic problem of my personal effort versus the power of God. It boils down to this: *granted that I want to do the will of God, what is the role of my human willpower and effort?*

When I was in high school and college, people used to assure me that I was trying too hard to be a good Christian. All I really had to do was "let go and let God." And I wanted to do exactly that. But let go of *what?* and let God do *what?* And *how* to let go? And *how* to let God? Nobody was very handy with the answers to those questions. In fact, I hardly dared frame the questions in my mind. They seemed impious and disrespectful. Anybody really *spiritual* wouldn't need to inquire.

I know that the same sort of advice is still being given to people in thousands of churches, schools, and homes. Very recently I heard a rather typical sermon on I Kings 2, where dying King David instructed Solomon to do away with Joab the son of Zeruiah. Joab represented the spirit of violence and the spirit of deceit, and David told Solomon to slay these immediately so that he could have a great reign. In the same way each of us in the congregation was instructed to put to death in himself the spirit of violence and deceit— of raging temper and hypocritical pretense.

Setting aside the question of the allegorical method, I waited eagerly for the real *meat* of the sermon: *how* this slaying should take place. But it was the same old "let go and let God" routine—the same old dodging of the human and reasonable responsibility involved. The congregation was reminded that Solomon had a strong man of war named Benaiah who did the actual killing on his behalf; and Benaiah stood for the Lord Jesus Christ. "Simply bring your Joabs to Jesus and let Him slay in you the spirit of violence and deceit."

Fine.

But how?

How?

Have I no role at all in the slaying of my own tendencies toward violence and deceit? Is it purely a matter of wishful thinking—"Jesus, do it for me," and lo! it is done? Experience has taught me otherwise.

Perhaps the best biblical summation of my quandary is located in Proverbs 3:5-6: "Trust in the Lord with all thine heart; and lean not unto thine own understanding. In all thy ways acknowledge him, and he shall direct thy paths." In what sense are *my* ways and *my* paths really *mine,* if they are directed by God without any effort of my own? And how does this direction take place? During my "let go and let God" days, I earnestly tried to become God's automaton,

but I found that He wouldn't cooperate. I tried in the way
that I saw a spiritualist medium on TV yield her body to
the ghost of Aaron Burr, letting him speak through her; but
God wouldn't cooperate. And I came increasingly to wonder
this: if I don't lean on my own understanding, upon whose
understanding should I lean? Am I not in perilous danger
of becoming the tool of any charismatic personality who
can convince me that he knows the mind of God better
than I do?

I recognize that if an individual rejects all authority, he
sets himself adrift at the mercy of his own whims—and may
soon find himself at the mercy of the whims of men more
powerful than himself. That is, I recognize the truth of what
C. S. Lewis wrote in *The Abolition of Man:*

> Either we are rational spirits obliged for ever to obey the
> absolute values of the *Tao* [Natural Law; the belief that
> certain attitudes are *really* true, and others *really* false] or else
> we are mere nature to be kneaded and cut into new shapes for
> the pleasures of masters who must, by hypothesis, have no
> motive but their own "natural" impulses. Only the *Tao* pro-
> vides a common human law of action which can overarch rulers
> and ruled alike. A dogmatic belief in objective value is neces-
> sary to the very idea of a rule which is not tyranny or an
> obedience which is not slavery.[2]

I must repeat that my whole soul recognizes the truth of
Lewis's statement. I can see that human beings degenerate
drastically when they view themselves as irresponsible
animals. Standing at the fresh grave of Senator Robert F.
Kennedy, that temporary plot a little to the left of his
President-brother's, that small receptacle of so much human
promise—standing in the Arlington silence and thinking of
America's recent rash of violence, I clearly recognize the
need for absolute, overarching ideals and standards. And I

am willing to equate these with the general will of God for the human race. But I am not the human race in general. I am only one member of it. I need to know the will of God for *me*. I am anxious to acknowledge God in all my ways, whatever that means, and to lean not unto my own understanding. How?

I can find no authority more solid, more time-tested, more psychologically realistic than that of the Bible. Certainly I can find no single source more likely to reveal to me the mind of God. I am painfully aware that I must be careful about claiming to know the mind of God, for I agree that "perhaps there is a two-fold danger with which any age of Christians must come to grips: either saying too much or saying too little, either presumptuous certainty about the divine activity or paralyzing humility about the impossibility of knowledge." [3] But seeking a balance between those extremes, I turn to the Bible for the light I need.

In all honesty I must confess that in addition to Proverbs 3:5-6, I find other passages which seem to imply an automated type of behavior that relieves me of all responsibility to think and act on my own. One of them is Psalm 37:5: "Commit thy way unto the Lord; trust also in him; and he shall bring it to pass." (I once knew a woman who was driven to divorce because her husband insisted on trusting in the Lord instead of honestly earning money to pay their bills). Or Psalm 44:6-7: "For I will not trust in my bow, neither shall my sword save me. But thou hast saved us from our enemies. . . ." (I wonder how long a soldier would survive in a Vietnam jungle if he took *that* literally?) Or Psalm 81:10: "Open thy mouth wide, and I will fill it." (I have met people who connected that promise with God's words to Moses in Exodus 4:12—"Now therefore go, and I will be with thy mouth, and teach thee what thou shalt say";

they claimed the promise for themselves, preached with inadequate preparation, and quite deservedly made fools of themselves.)

But there are also New Testament passages which stress the relaxed simplicity of doing God's will. The Apostle Paul declared that he did not even try to assess the justice or injustice of his own motives: "I judge not mine own self. For I know nothing by myself; yet am I not hereby justified: but he that judgeth me is the Lord" (I Cor. 4:3-4). I suppose that Jesus must have meant something like that when He said that in giving alms, I am not to let my left hand know what my right hand is doing (Matt. 6:3)—a literal impossibility, but figuratively an instruction about refraining from cataloguing my own virtues.

Then there are the many well-known passages which imply that learning and doing the will of God is a very simple matter of responding to the voice of God, of simply "walking in the light as he is in the light," without the slightest awareness of whether or not one is ultimately righteous. I remember that those who are to be blessed in the judgment of the sheep and goats (Matt. 25) do not even know that they are righteous, are not even aware that they have fed or clothed or housed or visited the Lord. They discover their own righteousness when Christ ultimately reveals it to them. And I suppose that this must mean they have very simply "let go and let God" live His life through them.

But wait a minute. There is another vein of emphasis in the Bible, a vein which is at the opposite extreme from the anti-intellectual, humanly passive vein I have been mining. Nothing could possibly require more strenuous intellectual effort than the injunction of I John 4:1: "Beloved, believe not every spirit, but try the spirits whether they are of God: because many false prophets are gone out into the world."

Or I Thessalonians 5:21: "Prove all things; hold fast that which is good." (No shrinking-violet attitude here; no "tell-me-whether-the-man-is-orthodox-before-I-listen-to-him"!)

Or take II Corinthians 13:5: "Examine yourselves whether ye be in the faith; prove your own selves." Strange advice that, from the same Apostle Paul who had written in his first letter to the same church that he did not judge himself but let the Lord judge him (I Cor. 4:3-4)! Unless I am willing to accuse St. Paul of manifest nonsense, which I am not willing to do, I must begin to concede that doing the will of God requires a paradoxical stance in which I simultaneously introspect and refrain from introspection, judge myself and others and refrain from judging myself and others.

Passages like Romans 12:2 make it sound as if learning and doing the will of God is an arduous mental process of examining circumstances and probing motives, for I am instructed to "prove what is that good, and acceptable, and perfect, will of God." And Philippians 1:9-11 is a prayer that the Christian's love may "abound yet more and more in knowledge and in all judgment; that ye may approve things that are excellent." And St. Luke praises the Berean Christians for using their minds to check up on the authority of Paul and Silas: "These [the Bereans] were more noble than those in Thessalonica, in that they received the word with all readiness of mind, and searched the scriptures daily, whether those things were so" (Acts 17:11). Yet I have met many a preacher and teacher who did not want his authority questioned; the most lauded students were the "simple souls" who showed their piety by believing whatever they were told.

There is, then, a vein of Scripture which stresses that knowing the will of God is an intellectual process involving shrewd discernment, sound thinking, and wise judgment. It is a challenging vein, and a necessary one, warning against the mystical sort of direct inspiration which can so easily become self-deception. In this connection I remember William Golding's novel *The Spire*. The main impression it gave me concerned the dangerous possibility of confusing egotistical desire with the will of God. The hero, Jocelin, had a consuming passion to erect an enormous spire on his cathedral. Never did I find a statement concerning whether the spire was actually God-inspired or ego-inspired; but I became increasingly uneasy as I witnessed the way Jocelin manipulated and sacrified human beings in order to achieve his dream.

I have admitted, so far, that I am challenged by the strain of Scripture which implies that knowledge of the will of God is achieved by honest intellectual effort. And I have admitted great confusion about the strain which implies that one can "let go and let God." But both strains are in the Bible, and I have accepted the Bible as a much-needed authority to shore against the ruins of my personal standards and the standards of society in general. I cannot therefore adopt the simple expedient of rejecting the one strain and accepting the other, unless I am willing to turn the Bible into a farcical supermarket in which I take what suits me and leave the rest. I must confess, though, that I have often seen it done that way. The people who urged me to "relax into the will of God," to "let go and let God," never once intimated that paradoxically opposite advice also appeared in the Bible. I would only be repeating their error if I sprang from one extreme to the other, rejecting the passive and relaxed side of Christianity in favor of the active and strenuous one.

Besides, the more I think about it, the more I can see

some truth in the "let go and let God" emphasis—as long
as it is counterbalanced by the "prove all things" emphasis.
I can see that if I lived my whole life feeling responsible to
prove all things, yet without any sense of the Holy Spirit of
God within me helping my spirit to make decisions, I might
become tortured by complexity, haunted constantly by
choices which are too delicate for me to make, paralyzed
into indecision by my fear of making the wrong choice and
thus offending a righteous God. If the Bible stressed nothing
except the discipline of choosing righteously, I would probably alternate between nervous desperation (when unsure
about what to do), self-hatred (when sure I had done
wrong), and self-righteousness (when sure I had done right).
Not being a psychologist, I really couldn't say which would
be the least healthy state of mind; but none of them seems
very healthy to me.

On the other hand, if the Bible stressed nothing but
simple obedience to the will of God, I might get involved
with the kind of spiritualizing which does not take into
account the pressures of everyday circumstances and practical reality. Or—and this is more likely for my temperament
—I might be unable to swallow the spiritualizing and thus
might erroneously decide that God has no interest in the
individual life and that Christianity is simply hokum.

But it is because the Bible paradoxically emphasizes both
poles of truth that I am likely to fall into error if I think
of the one without the other. Thus when I seek to trust in
the Lord with all my heart, and not lean on my own understanding, I must not repudiate my own insights, nor must I
refuse to make responsible decisions. Instead, I must judge
a human situation as carefully as I can, at the same time
reminding myself of my human limitations and the possibility of my own error. I must pray for God's guidance; I

must consciously open my thoughts to the influence of the Holy Spirit; I must try to see things as I think God might. see them, all the while aware that I am *not* God and that ego and self-interest might be skewing my judgment. As I swing into action, doing the thing which seems to be right in the situation so far as I can assess it, I must do so in reliance upon God's guidance and mercy; but I must not assume my own infallibility. I must perform my deed with a conscious acknowledgment of Him, in confidence that in fulfilment of His promise He will keep me from ultimately devastating error ("he shall direct thy paths"). At the same time, I am protected from a nervous breakdown by the knowledge that God knows my heart, and that I am acting with my trust in Him. If I am wrong in this individual case, He will apply to me the forgiveness made possible by Christ's redemptive death. So I am *simultaneously* resting in God and making responsible human choice.

In this sense it is true that a mature Christian bride and groom—I do not speak of the immature or irresponsible—have been brought together by God. The fault of the pastor who emphasized their obedience to the will of God lay in his failure to give equal emphasis to their human choice. They were simultaneously performing an act of responsible human will and letting God do His will in them. They were "letting go and letting God" in the sense that they recognized the limits of their human willpower and reason and were trusting in His guidance and consciously seeking His sanction. Yet they were acknowledging publicly that they had made a carefully considered choice and were willing to go all out to make it stick.

By the same token, when I commit my way to the Lord, I put forth all possible human effort to achieve the goal I have set for myself. But my trust is not in my effort; for all the while I know that no amount of effort will bring my goal to pass unless God so permits. If my goal is truly His will, there is no doubt that it will come to pass. But God is not my accomplice, under obligation to bring about just any goal I happen to set my mind on. There is always the margin of human error. I may think I am trusting purely in God, I may think my way is wholly committed to Him, yet be fooling myself completely. Redemption will cover such unconscious sin, for Christ "is able also to save them to the uttermost that come unto God by him, seeing he ever liveth to make intercession for them" (Heb. 7:25).

On the other hand, I must not assume that my every successful venture constitutes proof that God was in it. Psalm 37:5 does not promise tangible success, but only the fact that if I *will* to commit my way to God, He will bring about *genuine* commitment in my heart. He will take what was unreal and unaccustomed and turn it into a very real and meaningful habit: "he shall bring it to pass. And he shall bring forth thy righteousness as the light, and thy judgment as the noonday" (Psa. 37:5-6).

Furthermore, there may be times when I will judge myself a total failure even when I am not. Some people are psychologically too insecure ever to feel "in the will of God" for very long. That, too, is realistically covered by Scripture: "For if our heart condemn us, God is greater than our heart, and knoweth all things. Beloved, if our heart condemn us not, then have we confidence toward God" (I John 3:19-20). It is a beautiful thing to have full confidence of acting in the will of God—unless, of course, that confidence slips into self-righteousness. But the lack of that confidence does not necessarily mean that I am out of the will of God for me, because I am not the final judge of that. So I am back to the Apostle Paul's "I judge not mine own self . . . he that judgeth me is the Lord. Therefore judge nothing before the time. . . ."

When I am called upon to do intellectual or spiritual battle, I will carefully prepare my weapons but will not put my ultimate faith in the weapons, whether they be swords or arguments. I will prepare my lectures with painstaking care—but I will approach the platform with my ultimate faith pinned on the power of God rather than on my preparation and my ability. Thus at my best I am simultaneously a channel of responsible human effort and of an energy which lifts me above myself. To deny my responsible human effort would be a lie. To deny the power of the Holy Spirit in a Christian personality would also be a lie.

God's power? Human effort? When man is at his best, they cannot be distinguished. And in submission to the polarities of scriptural truth, I vow that I will not stress either factor to the exclusion of the other. For "according to Christian morality God is on both sides of the line; the will of God works *in* the wills of those who love him; and the grace of God is made known in the ability to love him." [4] Paul expressed the paradox in these words: "But by the grace of God I am what I am: and his grace which was bestowed upon me was not in vain; but I laboured more abundantly than they all: yet not I, but the grace of God which was with me" (I Cor. 15:10).

References for Chapter Two

¹ Dietrich Bonhoeffer, *Letters and Papers from Prison* (New York: Macmillan Paperbacks, 1965) , pp. 43-44. Copyright, 1953, by The Macmillan Company.
² C. S. Lewis, *The Abolition of Man* (New York: Collier Paperback, 1962), pp. 84-85.
³ James B. Nelson, "Contextualism and the Ethical Triad," in *The Situation Ethics Debate,* ed. Harvey Cox (Philadelphia: Westminster Press, 1968), p. 186.
⁴ A. Boyce Gibson, "Discussion of the Views of P. H. Newell-Smith," in *Christian Ethics and Contemporary Philosophy,* ed. Ian T. Ramsey (London: SCM Press Ltd., 1966), p. 123.

Three

. . . it is true that if all men acted on a rational basis and pursued their own interests rationally, there would be no conflict of interest; no one would seek to hurt another person, or to get anything—not even praise—which he had not earned. But of course that's a big **if.**

Chapter Three

SELF AND OTHERS

To get back to that much-praised formula for JOY—*Jesus*, *Others*, *Yourself*: how am I to be protected from exploitation if I literally follow such a formula? As I asked before, does living for *Others* mean systematically sacrificing my plans to theirs, my desires to theirs, my whole identity to theirs? If so, goodbye JOY!

I must, I suppose, ponder the alternatives. As far as I know, the only writer who has seriously espoused an ethics of "self first" is the founder of Objectivism, Ayn Rand. In her novels, *The Fountainhead* and *Atlas Shrugged*, she has shown such egoism in action. And in *The Virtue of Selfishness: a New Concept of Egoism*, she and her disciple Nathaniel Branden have argued uncompromisingly for selfishness, which they define as rational concern for one's own interests. Miss Rand attacks altruism as being "responsible, more than any other single factor, for the arrested moral development of mankind." [1] Accepting only a single reality, "the reality knowable to reason," [2] Miss Rand argues that "the *rational* interests of men do not clash," for "there is no conflict of interests among men who do not desire the unearned, who do not make sacrifices nor accept them." [3]

Miss Rand does not deny that a person might want to help those one loves; but she sees this assistance as *integrity* rather than "selflessness" or "sacrifice." Insisting that "morality is a code of black and white," [4] Rand and Branden argue that "a genuine selfishness—an uncompromising loyalty to one's judgment, convictions, and values—represents a profound moral achievement." [5] To these absolutists, there can be no such thing as a moral compromise: to say that life requires compromise is to say that "life requires the surrender of what is true and good to that which is false and evil." [6]

For Miss Rand, Christ's injunction to "judge not" must be changed to read "Judge, and be prepared to be judged." "Judge not" she regards as "an abdication of moral responsibility . . . a moral blank check one gives to others in return for a moral blank check one expects for oneself." [7] On the other hand, "to condemn without giving reasons is an act of irresponsibility, a kind of moral 'hit-and-run' driving." All in all, Miss Rand and Mr. Branden hold that a man should be "dispassionately and intransigently *fact*-centered," thinking and judging independently, "valuing nothing higher than the sovereignty of his intellect." [8]

Frankly, I don't think that any honest human being could shrug off Miss Rand's views as being complete nonsense. There is something attractive about the rigor with which she argues. And many of her insights are not only interesting but have the ring of truth. For instance, it is true that *if* all men acted on a rational basis and pursued their own interests rationally, there would be no conflict of interest; no one would seek to hurt another person, nor to get anything—

even praise—which he had not earned. But of course that's a big *if*.

It is also true that helping those one loves is far better categorized as integrity than as selfless sacrifice. To pick one obvious example, I think there is something diseased about seeing what I do for my child as self-sacrifice and thus building up in myself a martyr complex. Parents who regard themselves as martyrs for their children inevitably desire that later their children become martyrs for them: "I have done so much for you; the least you can do is get a job nearby," or "After all I've done to get you educated, how can you throw it all away marrying a person like that?" I must agree with Miss Rand (and with Robert Frost, who repeatedly introduces this idea into his poetry),[9] that what I do out of love is no self-sacrifice but something which I do freely because of what I am. And it therefore requires no repayment whatsoever.

Certainly Miss Rand and Mr. Branden are right in arguing that uncompromising loyalty to one's convictions, values, and judgment represents a profound moral achievement. So profound, in fact, that very few men have ever achieved it. But I frankly wonder whether this is an ideal which should even be encouraged, since it almost automatically causes anguish to the people surrounding any person who will not compromise on the slightest point.

I realize that what I am thinking will cause horror to many good people. But out with it. When I saw *A Man For All Seasons*, I came away from it deeply troubled. Not because I felt evil as compared to Thomas More's goodness, which would have been an expected reaction. No. Troubled because try as I might, I could not convince myself that More's refusal to compromise in that situation was really laudable. King Henry VIII had so arranged circumstances that More had to give only a very indirect consent to Henry's divorce, and More had already voiced his disapproval of the divorce so that everyone concerned was aware of his moral stand. But he could not yield the required reaction, passive as it was; and by thus maintaining the absolute whiteness of his own robes he condemned himself to death, his wife to widowhood, his whole family to exile, and England to a completely dishonest chancellor.

I was not surprised to see *A Man for All Seasons* lauded in the evangelical press for illustrating an excellent moral stand. And I think that Miss Rand would also praise St. Thomas More's action, for he acted out of absolute integrity, with no thought of self-sacrifice. Fine. But is no thought at all to be given to others, to the effect of my actions on society and especially on those I love? This is a subject which I must think more about.

To return to Miss Rand's views: her revision of "Judge not" to "Judge, and be prepared to be judged" is not as anti-Christian as it at first seems. Miss Rand is merely stressing one half of a biblical paradox, although I doubt she realizes that the New Testament contains any such paradox. For as surely as Matthew 7:1 and Luke 6:37 and Romans 2:1 contain the injunction to judge not, there are numerous New Testament passages which clearly instruct the believer to judge and be prepared to be judged. Take, for instance, I Corinthians 2:15: "But he that is spiritual judgeth all things." Or I Corinthians 6:2-3: "Do ye not know that the saints shall judge the world? and if the world shall be judged by you, are ye unworthy to judge the smallest matters? Know ye not that we shall judge angels? how much more things that pertain to this life?" Or I Corinthians 11:31: "For if we would judge ourselves, we should not be judged." Or Galatians 6:4: "But let every man prove [judge] his own work, and then shall he have rejoicing in himself alone, and not in another." Or I Thessalonians 5:21: "Prove [judge] all things; hold fast that which is good."

So there we are. The New Testament says that a Christian is to judge, yet to judge not. Pretty confusing. Yet Miss Rand's "correction" of Christ's statement illustrates the danger of overlooking the various polarities of truth in the Bible. The Bible is a big book, a realistic book, and when apparent contradictions exist it is time to notice both sides carefully and to bring them into meaningful balance with each other. A major weakness of Miss Rand's philosophy is that she achieves no such balance.

Examination of the "judge not" passages reveals that they are directed against repudiation of people, against making a final negative assessment of another person's worth. Because no limited human brain could possibly comprehend all the external and internal (conscious and unconscious) factors which have made a person what he is, no human being has the right to make ultimate judgment of another.

In this connection I think of Edith Wharton's powerful novelette, *Ethan Frome.* In it a farmer named Ethan Frome, married to a whining hypochrondriac named Zeena, quite understandably falls in love with his wife's warm, lively housekeeper, Mattie Silvers. When Zeena decides to send Mattie away, Ethan and Mattie go for a suicide run on a sled—but instead of killing themselves in the crash, they cripple themselves for life. The power of the novel lies in this: that at the end, Mattie has become the whining complainer that Zeena was at the beginning. I had disliked Zeena intensely; but I was able to be understanding and compassionate about Mattie. Why? *Because I understood how Mattie had gotten that way.* Edith Wharton was too good an artist to draw any overt morals, but the lesson is unforgettable through her excellent characterizations.

Furthermore, it is a commonplace of psychology that if a person is habitually judgmental of others, constantly making the final assessment—"he's dishonest to the core," "she isn't worth the time of day," and so forth—he reaps the fruit of bitterness in his own personality: "For with what judgment ye judge, ye shall be judged: and with what measure ye mete, it shall be measured to you again" (Matt. 7:2).

Examination of the "judge" passages indicates that they encourage precise evaluation of moral situations and human values, including the value of one's own work (although, as I discovered earlier, there *is* a paradoxical sense in which one can't judge his own work at all). It is on the basis of precise judgments that a person knows what action to take. So Miss Rand is not being as original and anti-biblical as she thought she was when she argued that man should strive to be "dispassionately and intransigently *fact*-centered," thinking and judging independently. But she errs when she thinks that total dispassion and intransigent factuality are possible for any actual individual. And she errs woefully when she thinks man should value "nothing higher than the sovereignty of his intellect."

The Bible is wiser than that.

My intellect is, in the first place, a gift from the Creator, and I rightly should value the Giver more than the gift. But my intellect has also been deformed so that it is far from being factually reliable. I have become increasingly aware as I have grown older that a person's intellect can so deceive him that he will bring into actual being something which began as objectively false or nonexistent. A person will accept a false definition, description, or explanation, but this falsehood will evoke "a new pattern of behavior which makes the originally false conception become true. The wish becomes father to the fact, the idea to the act." [10] This is exactly what occurs in John Millington Synge's drama, *The Playboy of the Western World:* because he accepts the people's erroneous acclaim of himself as a hero, the coward eventually becomes a hero. And Dr. Maxwell Maltz has, in his book *Psycho-Cybernetics,* given numerous real-life instances of the same process. So has John Holt, in *How Children Fail.*

In addition, there is the undeniable fact that very few people deliberately choose evil because they know it is evil and prefer evil. Many harmful acts spring from an ungovernable rush of passion; but where a motive can be discerned, "some twist of thought makes the worst appear the better reason; the act, looked at through the vapours of anger, fear, or jealousy, is seen in a false light." [11] The "reason" of many an assassin has betrayed him into insanity.

Where then is Miss Rand's "intransigently *fact*-centered" intellect? For that matter, even the "reality picture" held by any group of people is determined largely by the "conventional linguistic forms and receptacles for their thought," so that "unconscious linguistic patterns both shape our world and imprison our outlook." [12] And in a sense, language is always lying, "even where it strives for the greatest precision; it is never fully adequate to its referent." [13] Words and the things to which they refer cannot be perfectly matched.

Miss Rand is therefore simplistic to imagine that any human being is capable of objective factuality—or even that such fact-minded objectivity would be a healthy state of affairs. For as John Stuart Mill admitted in his *Autobiography,* once a person loses all power to feel, he loses all perception of values as well; he becomes "value-blind." [14] The achievement of goodness could never be an achievement of intellect alone—nor of emotion alone—but of both in a proper working balance. Which is exactly what I am seeking.

To summarize: Miss Rand's Objectivist philosophy contains a scattering of valuable insights upon a completely untenable and impracticable basis. Human beings are simply not capable of the rational objectivity she requires; and thus "the virtue of selfishness"—the virtue of a *totally rational* self-interest—is disqualified from the status of a workable philosophy of life.

But what about putting others before myself? This is certainly the theory under which I was reared, and it seems to be the New Testament way: "Let nothing be done through strife or vainglory; but in lowliness of mind let each esteem other better than themselves" (Phil. 2:3). The Sermon on the Mount is the classic on this subject: if anyone asks you for your coat, give him your cloak as well; if anyone asks you to go a mile with him, go two; give to him who asks, lend to him who wants to borrow. "Love your enemies, bless them that curse you, do good to them that hate you, and pray for them which despitefully use you, and persecute you" (Matt. 5:44). I was repeatedly instructed to base my moral and ethical decisions on injunctions like the following: "We then that are strong ought to bear the infirmities of the weak, and not to please ourselves. Let every one of us please his neighbor for his good to edification. For even Christ pleased not himself" (Rom. 15:1-3). Or "Abstain from all appearance of evil" (I Thess. 5:22).

But anybody who has seriously tried to put these passages into practice has encountered immediate and insuperable difficulties. As I think about these difficulties, they seem to fall into two major categories: first, the fact that many people would not be satisfied with my coat and my cloak but would take literally everything I had, either physically or psychically. At what point does one draw the line? Second, if I live to please others, and try to avoid everything which might upset others, won't I soon be unable to do *anything?* There are enough people in any one community to supply someone who will disapprove heartily of most things I do ("Women shouldn't go out to work," "Too much make-up," "That boy's hair is too long," "Good Christians don't go to the movies," and so forth) .

Robert Frost's poetry offers superb examples of the first dilemma—that is, how much an individual owes to a relative stranger as opposed to what he owes to himself and his own family. Warren faces such a decision in "The Death of the Hired Man," until Silas' death relieves him of making it. Silas had repeatedly sponged off Warren all winter and then when farmhands were really needed had gone off to work for someone who would offer him higher wages. How long should Warren have continued to allow such behavior at the expense of his own farm, his own family?

But the poem in which Frost puts the problem most directly is entitled "Love and a Question." A stranger comes to the door of a tiny cottage and seeks shelter for the night. The bridegroom who owns the cottage surveys the sky, recognizes that there will be a severe storm and that there is no other shelter in miles, yet can only think of his bride within, and of their mutual desire. The poem concludes without an answer:

> The bridegroom thought it little to give
>   A dole of bread, a purse,
> A heartfelt prayer for the poor of God,
>   Or for the rich a curse;
> But whether or not a man was asked
>   To mar the love of two

> By harboring woe in the bridal house
> The bridegroom wished he knew.[15]

Even Ayn Rand's rigid system offers no answer to that question. To a stranger, says Miss Rand, I owe only "the generalized respect and good will which one should grant to a human being in the name of the potential value he represents—until and unless he forfeits it."[16] But what if that stranger should single me out and ask my help, ask of me something which will hurt me or those I love? How far does charity reach? How high must I place the "potential value" the stranger represents?

It is of no use to be told simply to act upon what is *right*, as Miss Rand does; for it is precisely my problem that here I am not sure of what is right. I recognize that "self sacrifice is only required or justified where it is necessary in order to secure for another or others a *greater* good than that sacrificed," [17] but if I were that bridegroom how would I weigh the stranger's physical safety against getting my marriage off to a good start? Frost was very right not to answer the question he posed, for the answer to such a dilemma is agonizingly individual.

And then there is the problem of "the weaker brother." What does a passage like Romans 14:21 mean? "It is good neither to eat flesh, nor to drink wine, nor any thing whereby thy brother stumbleth, or is offended, or is made weak." Does that mean that I have to deny myself activities which I honestly believe are right for me, simply because someone else would disapprove or be hurt should he find out?

I know that many Christians interpret the doctrine of the weaker brother exactly this way. In fact, I remember hearing from his own lips how the president of a Christian college reacted to Romans 14. He had been staying overnight in Shakespeare country, in Stratford-on-Avon, England. Someone had presented him with a complimentary ticket to a Shakespearean production. He valued the plays of Shakespeare on the printed page and saw nothing wrong about seeing them produced on a stage; but because many of the constituents of his college back in America indiscriminately disapproved of theatre, he stayed alone in his room and read a book. He was proud of this incident because he felt it illustrated his submission to the doctrine of protecting the weaker brother.

But I wonder. No "weaker brother" was present to see what he was doing. He denied himself a positive good for the sake of a hypothetical somebody who might *possibly* have been unable to distinguish Shakespearean theatre from trash theatre. Was this a justifiable self-sacrifice? Was this necessary "in order to secure for another or others a *greater* good than that sacrificed"?

Don't misunderstand me: I am not passing judgment on the college president. More power to him if he did that which kept his conscience clear: "Happy is he that condemneth not himself in that thing which he alloweth" (Rom. 14:22). But I cannot see how he could have been consistent about such self-denial without completely impoverishing his life. Some people look down on those who drink coffee or Coca Cola; some think it immoral for men and women to go swimming together; others find it wrong to wear jewelry, even a watch. Does the Bible really require total abstinence from any thing which a *hypothetical* weaker brother might find unacceptable? In such a way, the "weaker brother" becomes the stronger brother, dictating his moral scruples for the obedience of everyone else.

I say hypothetical because I think it makes an enormous

difference whether or not the weaker brother is present at the time the act is committed. That is, if I were dining with a vegetarian who felt that eating flesh was ungodly, I would undoubtedly refrain from eating meat *while I was in his presence.* (I consider this nothing other than good manners). But I certainly would not feel it necessary to become a vegetarian for the sake of his conscience. As a matter of fact, I find this principle in the Bible itself. The passage in Romans 14 is chiefly about eating ceremonially unclean meat, or meat offered to idols: "For one believeth that he may eat all things: another, who is weak, eateth herbs" (vs. 2). Paul himself knew that nothing on earth is intrinsically evil; it becomes evil only if an individual's conscience sees it that way: "I know, and am persuaded by the Lord Jesus, that there is nothing unclean of itself: but to him that esteemeth anything to be unclean, to him it is unclean" (vs. 14).

But the conscience operates on the way it has been trained, so there are many times when a person needs to be *educated out of his narrowness,* charitably but firmly. (The Lord Jesus Himself must have had quite a time curing Paul of his scruples about unclean meats, for Paul had been "an Hebrew of the Hebrews, as touching the law, a Pharisee.") The actual educative process is illustrated in Acts 10:9-16, where Peter is shown a great sheet full of unclean animals. Told to rise, kill, and eat, Peter demurred: "Not so, Lord; for I have never eaten any thing that is common or unclean." And immediately he was corrected: "What God hath cleansed, that call not thou common." If Romans 14 were actually intended to say that all Christians should abstain from "unclean" meats because of the unenlightened consciences of a few, then surely a passage like Acts 10:9-16 would not appear in the Bible.

It seems to me that biblically there are several broad principles relevant to the "weaker brethren," who may be defined as "those defective in Christian intelligence." [18] Romans 14 stresses the need for living in loving compassion toward them, a compassion which might require occasional self-sacrifice for the sake of the unenlightened conscience. On the other hand, there are times when the weaker brother needs to be educated by the stronger one, as when Paul and Barnabas corrected the Jewish Christians who thought they still had to circumcise (Acts 15:1-2; cf. Gal. 5:1-15); or when Paul corrected the Christians who thought he should stay away from Jerusalem (Acts 21:12-14).

This latter principle has been underemphasized lately, especially in American evangelical circles. Christian college faculties have been forced to adopt policies which deprive their students of necessary educative contacts because of the fears of a largely uneducated constituency. While I recognize the need for patience and charity in such cases, I neverthe-less insist that the administration and faculty of these schools should be actively educating the conscience of their con-stituency, rather than trembling and retreating before their every whim.

So here again there is no simple rule of thumb in the Bible. There is no "in such a case, do this," and "in such a case, do that." There is on the one hand an injunction to refrain from eating flesh or drinking wine, or "any thing whereby thy brother stumbleth, or is offended, or is made weak" (Rom. 14:21). There is on the other hand the in-junction to "stand fast therefore in the liberty wherewith Christ hath made us free, and be not entangled again with the yoke of bondage" (Gal. 5:1).

How can a person do both at the same time? That is a balance which I must constantly strive to achieve. No one can tell me when I should give in to the scruples of my weaker brethren nor when I should stand fast in my Christian liberty and seek to reeducate their thinking. That is my decision and my responsibility.

Of one thing I am sure: I cannot live by one pole of truth and ignore the other without great peril to myself and others. If I stress only my liberty, I will become arrogant and lacking in compassion. If I stress only concern for others, I will become a slave to their ignorance. Paul sketches the necessary balance in Galatians 5:13-14: "For, brethren, ye have been called unto liberty; only use not liberty for an occasion to the flesh, but by love serve one another. For all the law is fulfilled in one word, even in this: Thou shalt love thy neighbour as thyself."

As thyself: here is no neurotic martyr-complex, no self-debasement, no sacrifice for others to an insane degree. And here is no self-sufficient tower of rationalistic egoism. Here instead is what Henry Hazlitt calls "mutualism" or "co-operativism," an interdependence of egoism and altruism, with each person considering the needs of all, including himself.[19] Somewhere I ran across an excellent illustration of the virtues of balance as opposed to the extremes of either egoism or altruism. If a building full of egoists were to catch on fire, many people would be trampled in the effort to get out the door first. If the building were full of altruists, many would be lost because everyone would be waiting for the other fellow to leave first. But if the building were full of people who had found a healthy balance between acceptance of their own value and respect for the value of others, they would leave as quickly as possible, without stampeding, and with a minimum loss of life.

Loving my neighbor as myself can mean nothing unless I learn never to treat myself as an exception to the standards

I expect others to meet—or, conversely, always to hold myself to the same set of rules by which I evaluate others. I am not thinking only of crisis situations, of momentous moral decisions, but also of the little daily acts which make up a life. Again I find myself in complete agreement with Henry Hazlitt: "Overemphasis on the contrast between manners and morals has blinded most writers on ethics from seeing that both manners and morals rest on the same underlying principle: sympathy, kindness, consideration for others." [20] It is certainly true that "Manners are minor morals," for as Emerson put it, "Good manners are made up of petty sacrifices." [21]

It is in the quiet routine of everyday life that a person's moral fiber is tested: does he phone home if he is unexpectedly delayed? does he give his hostess exact information about his arrival and departure so she will know how to plan? does he respect the privacy of others? does he apologize to children when he has misjudged them? Although a major crisis reveals a man's morality in a special way, there is a sense in which one could define every single day as a time that tries men's souls. For as Brand Blanshard writes,

> Any value or disvalue which, by being thrown into the scale, could affect a decision on right or wrong is of ethical moment. . . . The question whether to award a scholarship to X or Y is a moral problem. . . . The question whether, in one's will, one should leave money toward an art gallery, a college, or a playing field, is as truly a moral problem as the question whether one should tell a lie or break a promise. A question becomes a moral question at the moment when competing values, of any kind whatever, enter upon the scene.[22]

And that would include the competing values of keeping my comfortable bus seat versus offering it to an old lady who has nowhere else to sit.

In Search of Balance

Thoughtlessness is no excuse, either. It is the essence of immorality that it is either thoughtless or arrogantly mocking. Nevertheless, "In despising [or ignoring] moral value I despise myself. . . . Moral value is the scale by which I necessarily rate myself, unavoidably judge myself." [23] Christ said it this way: "For with what judgment ye judge, ye shall be judged: and with what measure ye mete, it shall be measured to you again" (Matt. 7:2). Because that is true, what could be more important than a constant concern for a just and proper balance between self-fulfilment and meeting the needs of others?

References for Chapter Three

[1] Ayn Rand, *The Virtue of Selfishness: a New Concept of Egoism* (New York: New American Library, 1964), pp. ix-x.

[2] Nathaniel Branden, in Rand, p. 39.

[3] Rand, p. 28.

[4] Rand, p. 102.

[5] Branden, in Rand, p. 73.

[6] Rand, p. 88.

[7] Rand, p. 91.

[8] Branden, in Rand, p. 188.

[9] See "A Tuft of Kelp," "Two Tramps in Mud-Time," and other poems.

[10] Paul Kurtz, *Decision and the Condition of Man* (Seattle: University of Washington Press, 1965), p. 96.

[11] Brand Blanshard, *Reason and Goodness* (London: George Allen and Unwin Ltd., 1961; 2nd ed., 1966), p. 342.

[12] Kurtz, p. 188.

[13] Rosalie L. Colie, *Paradoxia Epidemica: The Renaissance Tradition of Paradox* (Princeton: Princeton University Press, 1966), p. 516.

[14] Blanshard, p. 54.

[15] Robert Frost, "Love and a Question," in *Complete Poems of Robert Frost* (New York: Henry Holt, 1959), pp. 9-10. Copyright 1934 by Holt, Rinehart and Winston, Inc. Copyright © 1962 by Robert Frost. Reprinted by permission of Holt, Rinehart and Winston, Inc.

[16] Rand, p. 52.

[17] Henry Hazlitt, *The Foundations of Morality* (Princeton: D. Van Nostrand Co., 1964), p. 113.

[18] George Williams, *The Students' Commentary on the Holy Scriptures* (Grand Rapids: Kregel Publications, 1949), p. 872.

[19] Hazlitt, p. 103.

[20] Hazlitt, p. 75.

[21] Hazlitt, pp. 75-77.

[22] Blanshard, p. 324.

[23] Austin Fagothey, S. J., *Right and Reason: Ethics in Theory and Practice* (St. Louis: C. V. Mosby Co., 1963), p. 75.

Four

Here . . . is the principle that things are subordinate
to people; a Christian's clean conscience or sense
of self-righteousness is only a thing as compared
to the need of others.

Chapter Four

RELATIVISTIC ABSOLUTISM

After so much theorizing, I should probably put myself to the task of thinking through a concrete method for moral decisions. Nothing disturbs me more than a simple-minded, naïve use of the Bible to justify whatever a person wants to do, and I want to take every possible step to assure that I will not be guilty of such blasphemy. You don't have to know much history to be aware that the Bible has been used to support all sorts of atrocious activities—and at the moment I am thinking of the institution of slavery.

Stephen Vincent Benét's poem *John Brown's Body* offers a powerful example. Benét writes of a slave-ship captain who has sent for his first mate. As the mate enters, the captain first closes his Bible carefully, "putting it down/ As if his fingers loved it." Then he turns and addresses the mate with a shadow in his eyes: "I think, while this weather lasts," he says, "We'd better get them on deck as much as we can." The reason for his decision is a purely materialistic one:

"They keep better that way." And besides, he adds without smiling, the ship has begun to stink already. As the mate leaves the cabin to execute his orders, he hears the sound of the Bible being opened again.

Later, when the captain notices that the mate is getting thoroughly sick of his job, he admits that he knows of songs which have been made in criticism of him as the man who "traded in niggers and loved his Saviour." Says the captain,

> "They mean it bad but I don't take it bad.
> I get my sailing-orders from the Lord."
> He touched his Bible. "And it's down there, Mister,
> Down there in black and white—the sons of Ham—
> Bondservants—sweat of their brows."
> His voice trailed off
> Into texts. "I tell you, Mister," he said fiercely,
> "The pay's good pay, but it's the Lord's work, too."

Meanwhile, down in the hold, some of the slaves are thinking of themselves in terms of captive Israel, and are singing,

> "Won't you send me a pro-phet
> Just one of your prophets
> Like Moses and Aaron
> To get me some bail?"

The slave-ship captain was using the Bible to justify his actions. He was taking the curse Noah put upon Ham, the father of Canaan—"a servant of servants shall he be unto his brethren" (Gen. 9:25)—and applying it to the black people, but without the slightest evidence that they are the descendants of Canaan or of Ham, or that the same curse would be active after so many centuries. He also mixed in the curse of God on Adam—"in the sweat of thy face shalt thou eat bread" (Gen. 3:19)—which, to be logical, would then indicate that *all* mankind should be sold into slavery. In short, he was using the Bible to rationalize his own lucrative sin. I am frightened by the fact that he was perfectly sincere in imagining himself the servant of the Lord. Frightened because I can conceive the possibility of manipulating the Bible to make it mean what I want it to mean. In my own lifetime I have seen dreadful examples of cruel actions perpetrated with a handful of proof-texts to provide "sanction."

On the other hand, the slaves in the hold of the ship were allegorizing the Old Testament in order to see themselves as the Israelites in captivity to Egypt, with the hope of a Moses-deliverer. I can see an obvious danger here: through allegory, any Old Testament passage could be made to mean almost anything at all. In the case of the slaves who used the allegory to give themselves a hope of freedom, the allegorization was harmless. But I shudder to think of what would happen should, say, some twentieth-century Black Power Movement extend the allegory and decide to bring down its own set of plagues on the United States, or drown American citizens in a modern Red Sea.

This leaves me, of course, thinking about what the Bible *does* say about the relationship between white and black races. I know that Genesis 9:25 is not the only one which has been taken as supporting white supremacy. The fact that St. Paul sent Philemon's slave Onesimus back to his master has been cited as an approval of a slave-society; but since there is no proof and very little possibility that Onesimus was a black man, this proves nothing except that the Bible was written within certain historical contexts and must be interpreted primarily within those contexts. In Philemon I think it is obvious that St. Paul knew he couldn't change existing society overnight, but also that the gospel he was preaching would eventually change the structure of that society. In the meantime he worked within the system toward the most Christian immediate solution possible, asking the master to receive the slave "not now as a servant, but above a servant, a brother beloved. . . . If thou count me therefore a partner, receive him as myself" (Philemon 16-17). The "receive him as myself" certainly implies that Paul expected Philemon to free Onesimus, since Philemon would not attempt to hold the Apostle Paul in bondage.

Society's structure has changed since the book of Philemon was written. Taking cognizance of these changes, I conclude that Philemon instructs modern man to receive downtrodden people as beloved brethren, as partners, and as fellow laborers, not as inferior in any way except in opportunity—which it is our responsibility to provide.

But immediately I remember hearing I Peter 2:18 used to justify the maintenance of the status quo: "Servants, be subject to your masters with all fear; not only to the good and gentle, but also to the froward." Opponents of civil rights argue that this passage requires passivity in the downtrodden; that it is wrong for people to rebel against their lot and try to improve their way of life by making demands of the "masters," those who are better off. But I doubt that such is the meaning. It seems to me that Peter is here counseling subjection to one's *unchangeable* fate because this is, realistically, the only way to stay sane. But the passage must be interpreted in context to be accurately understood.

The widest context of any biblical passage is the *whole* Bible and the whole *accumulated experience of mankind.* The Bible cannot be studied in a vacuum, for theological principles remain irrelevant until they are related to the events of the contemporary world. Harvey Cox points out that during the 40's and 50's, theology had overreacted to sentimentalized religious experience and had focused on the objective *Word* of God rather than on *experience* of Him. Bultmann stressed absolute obedience to God; Reinhold Niebuhr stressed man's proneness to self-deception in his ethical thinking. But the Second Vatican Council and the "death of God" controversy ended that chapter, for the appeal of the radical theologians is rarely to Scripture, tradition, or doctrinal history—it is to experience. Fletcher's *Situation Ethics* arrived just in time to encourage the tendency to "return to experience." [2] But my point here is that a balance must be sought between reliance solely on the words of the Bible and reliance solely on human experience. The Bible gives meaning to experience, and experience gives meaning to the Bible. Each is the context of the other.

Taking I Peter 2:18 in this whole context, I conclude that there is a paradox which must be recognized. The immediate context is "Fear God. Honor the King. Be subject to your masters. If you suffer for goodness' sake, and bear it patiently, God will bless you." But the larger context of the whole Bible and of human experience indicates that while it is *usually* best to obey one's physical, environmental, and governmental masters, there are some notable exceptions. Jochebed, for instance, disobeyed civil authorities by preserving her son Moses; Rahab betrayed her own government by assisting the spies from Canaan; Daniel disobeyed the king's decrees; Jeremiah spoke boldly against government policies. All of them were blessed by God for their varying degrees of civil disobedience. And in the context of human experience, I remember that Martin Luther rebelled against his Roman Catholic masters and gave us the Reformation. I remember too that when many Germans *failed* to rebel against their Nazi masters they contributed to the slaughter of millions of Jews.

In Search of Balance

The other biblical passage used by many Christians to condemn all revolutionary activity (including even the mildest expression of student antagonism to administrators, to say nothing of civil rights demonstrators) is Romans 13:1-7:

> Let every soul be subject unto the higher powers. For there is no power but of God: the powers that be are ordained of God. Whosoever therefore resisteth the power, resisteth the ordinance of God: and they that resist shall receive to themselves damnation. . . . Render therefore to all their dues: tribute to whom tribute is due; custom to whom custom; fear to whom fear; honour to whom honour.

This passage is expressed in absolute terms because it is ordinarily the wisest and most honorable course of action. But it was never written to evoke the mindless obedience by which many Christians save themselves the trouble of involvement; it was written by the Apostle Paul, who was often in jail for his refusal to obey government officials by ceasing to spread the gospel.

Furthermore, in the context of the whole Bible I cannot forget the story of the Good Samaritan. Those who refused to help the man who fell among thieves refused in order to keep their own robes white and clean. In the same fashion, many contemporary Christians assume that *just as long as their private lives are pure,* all is well. Again and again at the Nurenberg Trials, the excuse was offered, "I only acted under orders"—as if obedience to government were the only value on earth. And again and again in America, attempts to accelerate social change receive blanket condemnation because even the slightest infraction of the law is regarded as violating the truth of Romans 13:1-7 and I Peter 2:18. But obviously, I must seek a balance between the value taught in these passages, and the values illustrated elsewhere in the Bible and human experience.

I do not mean to imply that the story of the Good Samaritan compels everybody to carry placards and join in Civil
Rights marches—or to participate to the neck in any other
specific social movement. *How* a person becomes involved is
a matter of personal, private conviction, temperament, and
opportunity. But I feel sure that the accumulated evidence
of the Bible and human experience indicates that *the true
follower of Christ must be involved in helping the downtrodden.*

St. James defines "pure religion and undefiled before
God and the Father" as twofold: "to visit the fatherless and
widows in their affliction, and to keep himself unspotted
from the world" (1:27). The "fatherless and widows" in the
Bible's social setting represented the disadvantaged, the
downtrodden, the forgotten. And "the world" in the New
Testament context represents the self-centered philosophy
of uncurbed, unregenerate mankind. So "pure religion,"
according to St. James, is being *actively* concerned about
the downtrodden, and consciously at war with my own
tendencies toward self-aggrandizement.

I must think through a single situation more concretely.
Suppose I were asked to participate in a civil rights sit-in
which will mildly break the law. I choose civil rights because
it is the number one domestic issue as I write; and I speak
of *mild* law-breaking because I believe that violence is
almost never right. (As I was about to say violence is *never*
right, I thought of the attempt upon Hitler's life in which
Dietrich Bonhoeffer participated. Had it succeeded, I wonder
how many other lives would have been spared?)

At any rate, I am asked to participate in the sit-in, and I
wonder whether I should do so, even though in this particular case I am sure that the cause is righteous. There is an
unjust law of such long-standing that the public is insensi-

tive to its injustice; all ordinary channels have been tried. How am I to respond? What is God's will for me? How can I know?

I might respond in any one of three ways. First, I might enthusiastically join in the law-breaking, refusing to recognize that there is any guilt involved. After all, I might reason, if one law is unfair then I am within my rights to break other laws. But this seems to me an irresponsible reaction, for an occasional unjust law cannot be used to invalidate the whole structure of social order.

Second, I might choose to hide legalistically behind the biblical passages telling the Christian to be subject to the powers that be. Exonerating myself from all guilt concerning unjust laws, I might rationalize that as long as my private life is pure, it is none of my business what happens on the governmental level. But this position is as irresponsible as the first. Nowhere in the New Testament do principles come before *persons;* in fact, when He was challenged about breaking the principle of the Sabbath for the good of His disciples, Christ reminded the Pharisees that David also had violated the law because of human need. He then made the classic statement of the subordination of things (including principles) to people: "The sabbath was made for man, and not man for the sabbath" (Mark 2:23-28).

Third, I might thoughtfully examine the situation and seek Christ's purpose for me in that situation. Knowing that I must respond to what Christ impresses me to do, even if that should mean breaking one law in order to serve a higher law, I must find a proper balance for me in that particular situation. I must not overlook the fact of my responsibility to duly constituted authority, for I take as my general moral maxim that I should "Always follow the established moral rule, always abide by my prima facie duty, unless there is a clear reason for not doing so." [3] But on the other hand, I must not be afraid to recognize and act upon that clear reason when it comes along.

How nervous David must have felt when he ate the holy showbread, "which is not lawful to eat but for the priests"! Strict observances were connected with the tabernacle, and the results of tampering with anything in it were dreadful, as when over fifty thousand people of Beth-shemesh were killed for inadvertently looking upon the ark of the Lord (I Sam. 6:19). David must have felt great fear, to say nothing of his reluctance about breaking a law so thoroughly ingrained in him from his youth up. But he and his men were desperately hungry, and in confidence that it was God's will for him to break the law in that situation, he ate of the showbread and gave it to his men as well.

And how totally upset must Abraham's categories have become when he was told to sacrifice his son Isaac! Aside from his personal anguish, which must have been enormous, how morally confused he must have felt! His God was not a pagan god who demanded human sacrifice. This command went against any of Abraham's previous experience of how a man was expected to live. Yet he was willing to go ahead with what he had been commanded to do, for he valued the command of God more highly than his previous moral categories.

To get back to my case of the civil rights sit-in: feeling that because of the righteousness of the cause I would be doing the will of God by breaking a human law in this special case (say, helping to block traffic by sitting on a certain street), I would not dare to make light of the law itself. I would incur a certain human guilt out of love for Christ who bore the guilt of the world. I would recognize that, although my heart condemned me for what I was doing, yet "God is greater than our heart, and knoweth all things" —and after all my heart would condemn me even more for *refusing* to help what I believed to be a righteous cause. I would sin because in that situation I had to sin; and I would feel guilt; but I would plead the redemption.

This surely must be the attitude of a thoughtful Christian fighting in Vietnam: he breaks God's law ("Thou shalt not kill") in order to uphold a government which regards human life as sacred and in order to combat a government in which human life is cheap. He must break God's law on one level to obey it on another. Yet he cannot kill another man lightly, and must commit his pangs of guilt into the hands of God.

I must bear in mind that Christ once sacrificed a whole herd of swine to restore the sanity of two maniacs at Gadara, and the swine were the property of somebody else! This was, humanly speaking, a violation of property laws in order to meet a desperate human need. Here again is the principle that things are subordinate to people; a Christian's clean conscience or sense of self-righteousness is only a thing as compared to the need of others. I must learn to be open to the will of God, not blocking His guidance by prefabricated prescriptions of my own. And in plain terms I think that this means I must be sensitive to the nuances of a situation and to the human need around me.

No doubt I will be accused of espousing situation ethics by people who totally repudiate the new morality. Well, I must at the outset admit that in this I agree with Joseph Fletcher, author of *Situation Ethics:* "Only the unwary will be taken in by the pseudobravery and bogus prophetic courage of those who drive ahead to an ideal regardless of the pain or price involved. It is right or wrong to follow a principle only according to who gets hurt and how much." [4]

(Here is the explanation for my difficulties with *A Man for All Seasons*).[5]

I have said that I agree with Fletcher here, and I do in the main; yet immediately I notice an area of slight disagreement. The word *only* bothers me. Because I am human and limited in knowledge, I cannot be *sure* of who will get hurt or how much, and I therefore feel wary of making this my sole basis for judgment. Rather I must put what I know about the situation into the scales, but must put biblical moral principles into the scales as well. I must ask, does this situation really necessitate the violation of a revered, time-tested, authoritative principle? Am I ready to incur the inevitable guilt involved in such a violation? Does a still small voice within tell me that in this situation, this is what I am to do? Here as always, I am in search of balance.

Bonhoeffer said it this way: "Responsibility implies tension between obedience and freedom. . . . The man of responsibility stands between obligation and freedom; he must dare to act under obligation and in freedom; yet he finds his justification neither in his obligation nor in his freedom but solely in Him who has put him in this (humanly impossible) situation and who requires this deed of him. The responsible man delivers up himself and his deed to God." [6]

One of the reviewers of *Situation Ethics* put into words what many people are thinking about both that book and the whole issue of new morality: "Fletcher's brand of Christian ethics is either an incarnation of Luther's 'sin bravely,' or it is Evil quoting Scripture for its own purposes." [7] I agree with that reviewer in leaning toward the first interpretation, but I think that any sensitive person must often distrust his own motives and question himself about the possibility of becoming a wolf in sheep's clothing.

I do have a basic quarrel with Fletcher, whose work I nevertheless admire for its passionate honesty. As I have already implied, I think he is wrong to deny the guilt involved in breaking a moral law because of the needs of a specific situation. Guilt inevitably (rightly or wrongly, consciously or unconsciously) accompanies the deserting of any values a person has been taught all his life. It may be a *false* guilt, but it feels like guilt all the same. Remember how Huckleberry Finn felt when he lied in order to assist Negro Jim's escape from slavery? It was Huck's "coming of age"; it was the best thing he had ever done; it was his assumption of responsibility—but at the time he was so burdened with guilt that he was sure he had damned his soul for eternity. He was siding with a black man against his own race; he was violating property rights; he was going against everything he had been taught was decent. He was sure of damnation. In fact, the beauty of his action lies right there: that Huck was *willing* to be damned, if necessary, for the sake of his friend.

Fletcher tells about the reaction of the French resistance fighters during World War II. They lived by means of lies, theft, and killing, sometimes even killing one of their own members if his arrest and possible defection were imminent possibilities. Asked about their morals, the *maquis* replied: "Everything is permitted—and everything is forbidden." Their interviewer took this to mean that "if killing and lying are to be used it must be under the most urgent pressure of social necessity, and with a profound sense of guilt that no better way can be presently found." But Fletcher demurs; he thinks that the word *guilt* should be changed to *sorrow*, "since such tragic situations are a cause for regret, but not for remorse." [8]

It seems to me, however, that Fletcher has forgotten the

difference between repentance and remorse. For a Christian the appropriate response to guilt is not remorse—not the despairing self-hatred which sent Judas out to hang himself—but repentance, which returns to Christ for cleansing and forgiveness as Peter returned after his betrayal.

I believe that any time a person exercises his Christian liberty and acts in any way contrary to what he has recognized as a moral rule, he will feel guilt. He may be choosing the lesser evil, but he will still be aware of choosing evil and will be distressed about that. Fletcher thinks this is preposterous: "Intrinsicalism sometimes results in stigmatizing as a 'lesser evil' such loving deeds as stealing a man's gun to keep him from shooting somebody in anger." [9]

But stealing a man's gun *is* evil, even though it is clearly the lesser evil in the case Fletcher proposes. To deny that it is evil will not take away the guilt associated with violating the principle of property rights. My loving motive makes me willing to assume the guilt as part of my responsible activity. But to deny that there *is* any guilt is to shrug off part of my responsibility. To deny the presence of guilt is also to deny reality by repressing my conscience, a very dangerous practice. And to deny guilt is to lose the opportunity to experience grace.

After all, guilt is not the same thing as *condemnation*. "There is therefore now no condemnation to them which are in Christ Jesus" (Rom. 8:1), but there is no such promise about guilt. To a mature Christian, feelings of guilt are signals that it is time to plead the redemption, time for conscious immersion in the forgiveness Christ made possible by his death. And thus "by degrees the awareness of our guilt and of God's love increase side by side. 'It is the saints who have a sense of sin, . . . the sense of sin is the measure of a soul's awareness of God'." [10] I cannot see how, under

Fletcher's attitude of "no guilt involved," a person could grow to a fully mature appreciation of redemption in Christ.

To summarize: I agree with James B. Nelson that "the moral actor may need to pray for God's forgiveness in the very moment that he is, to the best of his understanding, responding faithfully to God's claim upon him." [11] And with Dietrich Bonhoeffer that "the suspension of the law can only serve the true fulfillment of it. In war, for example, there is killing, lying, and expropriation solely in order that the authority of life, truth and property may be restored. A breach of the law must be recognized in all its gravity. . . . Whether an action arises from responsibility or from cynicism is shown only by whether or not the objective guilt of the violation of the law is recognized and acknowledged, and by whether or not, precisely in this violation, the law is hallowed." [12] Think how guilty many of the founders of America must have felt when they committed treason against the crown they had served all their lives! They pledged their lives, their fortunes, and their sacred honor to the course of action they felt they must follow; and that's exactly what they would have paid had they lost the Revolutionary War. They would then have been remembered not as patriots, but as traitors. And how thankful I am for their courage, for I like all Americans have profited by their willingness to lay their reputations on the line. Suppose they had been too concerned about their sacred honor to take the risk?

I have titled this essay "Relativistic Absolutism." I might just as well have used Fletcher's phrase, "Principled Relativism," except for the difference in emphasis. Human nature being as self-deceptive as it is, I think the emphasis must go on the principles, the absolutes, rather than on the relativistic freedom. I must insist again on my difference from Fletcher: whereas he argues that a loving purpose makes a lie *right,* I am convinced that the lie remains wrong in principle even when the situation forces a righteous man to use it. I say this in full cognizance of I Corinthians 6:12 and 10:23, which Fletcher cites: "All things are lawful unto me, but all things are not expedient: all things are lawful for me, but I will not be brought under the power of any." I think St. Paul means that when a man perceives in a certain case that he must transcend ordinary law for a higher law, what he does is "lawful" in the sense that it is God's will for him at that moment; yet he nevertheless violates ordinary law. So he simultaneously obeys the higher law and needs to seek forgiveness for violating the lower one. And all the while, he must be careful not to come under the power of his own deceptive will, which might lead him to think that transcending the natural law in one point gives him license to ignore it in other cases.

Milton's drama *Samson Agonistes,* based on Judges 13-16, provides an excellent illustration of this point. Manoa was unwilling to get the girl of Timna for Samson's wife, not because he disliked her, but because he was trying to hold out for the Hebraic law recorded in Deuteronomy 7:1-4, forbidding the marriage of Israelites with pagan women. Samson, however, knew from "intimate impulse" (private inspiration) that he was supposed to marry her. Milton's presentation follows the biblical account very exactly: "But his father and his mother knew not that it was of the Lord" (Judges 14:4). Here is another clear-cut biblical example of God's directing a man to break one of His own laws. But Milton also presents the *danger* of private inspiration, for when Samson desires Dalila he assumes that what was God's will in one context is God's will in another. Later, when he has faced the fact that his relationship with Dalila was his own will and without sanction, Samson admits what had happened: "I thought it lawful from my former act." [13] Nevertheless, the validity of private inspiration is reestablished when Samson recognizes that he is to go willingly to the feast of Dagon in spite of Hebrew laws forbidding such attendance. And there God does a mighty work through him.

I recognize that my difference of emphasis—"Relativistic Absolutism" rather than "Principled Relativism"—is only that: a difference of emphasis. For after all, Fletcher does state that "The situationist enters into every decision-making situation fully armed with the ethical maxims of his community and its heritage, and he treats them with respect as illuminators of his problems." [14] But I would say rather that I should have *so much* respect for ethical maxims that I would depart from a general principle only when forced by unique circumstances to make a great leap. And that leap had *better* be a leap in faith!

I. M. Crombie points out that there are two kinds of rigidity and two kinds of elasticity—of *interpretation,* in which moral rules are always valid but are elastic in interpretation (this is not really a lie; this is love) and of *application,* in which moral rules are not necessarily always valid but are rigid in interpretation (I shouldn't ever lie, but in this case I must).[15] Obviously, Fletcher's is an elasticity of interpretation while mine is an elasticity of application. But I think we would both have to agree with Iris Murdoch that we must steer a middle course between the "hidebound inflexibility" of a person who never adjusts rules to situations, and the "neurotic indetermination" of a person who always hesitates in the fear that he has not fully understood the situation. "To steer the middle course," says Miss Murdoch, "is itself a moral choice." [16]

Yes. And I choose to call my middle course by the name

of relativistic absolutism: *relativistic* because of human limitation and the complexity of various situations in which men find themselves; *absolutism* because of my enormous respect for the practical principles known to all men by reason, by tradition, and by Revelation.

References for Chapter Four

[1] Stephen Vincent Benét, *John Brown's Body* (New York: Holt, Rinehart and Winston, Inc., 1928). Copyright, 1927, 1928 by Stephen Vincent Benét. Copyright renewed, 1955, 1956, by Rosemary Carr Benét. Reprinted by permission of Brandt & Brandt.

[2] Harvey Cox, "Introduction and Perspective," in *The Situation Ethics Debate*, ed. Harvey Cox (Philadelphia: Westminster Press, 1968), pp. 16-18.

[3] Henry Hazlitt, *The Foundations of Morality* (Princeton: D. Van Nostrand, 1964), p. 184.

[4] Joseph Fletcher, *Situation Ethics* (Philadelphia: Westminster Press, 1966), p. 144.

[5] See above, p. ——.

[6] Dietrich Bonhoeffer, *Ethics*, ed. Eberhard Bethge (New York: Macmillan paperback, 1955), p. 254. Copyright © 1955 by the Macmillan Company.

[7] George Roleder, "Review of *Situation Ethics*," in *The Situation Ethics Debate*, ed. Harvey Cox, p. 66.

[8] Fletcher, p. 124.

[9] Fletcher, p. 125.

[10] Paul Tournier, *Guilt and Grace: A Psychological Study* (New York: Harper and Row, 1962), p. 160.

[11] James B. Nelson, "Contextualism and the Ethical Triad," in *The Situation Ethics Debate*, ed. Harvey Cox, p. 183.

[12] Bonhoeffer, *Ethics*, pp. 261-262.

[13] John Milton, *Samson Agonistes*, line 231; and see lines 307-314 on the subject of God's freedom to transcend His own laws. In *John Milton: Complete Poems and Major Prose*, ed. Merritt Y. Hughes (New York: Odyssey, 1957), pp. 557-559.

[14] Fletcher, p. 26.

[15] I. M. Crombie, "Moral Principles," in *Christian Ethics and Contemporary Philosophy*, ed. Ian T. Ramsey (London: SCM Press Ltd., 1966), p. 236.

[17] Iris Murdoch, "Vision and Choice in Morality," in *Christian Ethics and Contemporary Philosophy*, p. 209.

Five

Aristotle discusses the principle of morality as a balance between extremes of excess and defect, and leaves every man alone in each concrete situation—alone to decide precisely **where** for him the balance lies, alone to make his terrible choices.

Chapter Five

THE GOLDEN MEAN

There is really nothing very new about where my thoughts have led me. After all, it was thousands of years ago that the Preacher wrote, "The thing that hath been, it is that which shall be; and that which is done is that which shall be done: and there is no new thing under the sun. Is there any thing whereof it may be said, See, this is new? it hath been already of old time, which was before us" (Ecclesiastes 1:9-10).

Much more recently a scholar has written that after 2500 years of ethical treatises, even a professional philosopher could not be expected to come up with a completely original theory of ethics. Progress can still be made, but it probably consists in "more definiteness, precision, and clarification, in harmonization, in more generality and unification." [1]

I am no philosopher; but I have been attempting to find my own balance, to harmonize and unify my own vision of reality. It is all very well for Thoreau to tell me to march to the cadence of my own drummer; but I must first sensitize my hearing and learn to distinguish my own drummer from everyone else's. And perhaps more times than non-conformist Thoreau ever realized, I may find that when I am on balance, my cadence harmonizes with that of others.

About 2300 years ago a philosopher named Aristotle delivered to his Lyceum students a lecture series which has formed the basis for a great treatise, *The Nichomachean Ethics,* named after Aristole's father, Nicomachus. In these lectures I find an enormous concern for balance: "Just behavior is the mean [or point of balance] between doing injustice and suffering it." [2]

Aristotle, concerned with practical ethics rather than with arid theories, did not minimize the complex pressures which make balance difficult in specific situations. In fact he summarizes the heart of his ethics by reference to those difficulties:

> Moral excellence is a mean . . . a mean between two forms of badness, one of excess and the other of defect, and is so described because it aims at hitting the mean point in feelings and in actions. This makes virtue hard of achievement, because finding the middle point is never easy. . . . It is easy to fly into a passion—anybody can do that—but to be angry with the right person and to the right extent and at the right time and with the right object and in the right way—that is not easy, and it is not everyone who can do it.[3]

Which may well be the greatest understatement since the fourth century B.C.!

Brand Blanshard has scorned Aristotle's rule of conduct, "nothing in excess," as "almost scandalously vague." [4] But it seems to me that the "vagueness" (which I would call elasticity) is what is most meaningful in Aristotle. He does not give simplistic formulae, for he knows that no human context is entirely the same as any other. Rather, he discusses the principle of morality as a balance between extremes of excess and defect, and leaves every man alone in each concrete situation—alone to decide precisely *where* for him the balance lies, alone to make his terrible choices. To be less vague would be to set up rigid rules which would snap under the pressure of real situations. Aristotle is as vague and as challenging as the modern existentialists.

As a matter of fact, Aristotle could almost qualify as a situation ethicist, for he says that "the truly good and wise man . . . bears with dignity all that fortune sends him and invariably takes the most honorable line of conduct *that is open to him in the circumstances"* (italics mine). Apparently he felt, unlike Joseph Fletcher, that even when a man does the best he can, he may still be incurring guilt, for his advice is to *"keep away from that extreme which is the more opposed to the mean. . . .* For one of the extremes is always a more dangerous error than the other; and—since it is hard to hit the bull's-eye—we must take the next best course and choose the least of the evils." [6] In other words, Aristotle counsels that each man must decide which extreme poses more danger to a man of his temperament; and he must lean toward the *safer* evil in order to keep on as even a keel as he can. But he recognizes evil as evil; no situation can turn it to good. As a matter of fact, he goes so far as to distinguish processes which are bad absolutely and yet are acceptable relatively: "Sometimes, though they are bad absolutely, they will not be bad relatively; nay, for a particular person they will be positively desirable. And some processes, not even desirable for him generally, are desirable for an individual on occasion and for a time, though not absolutely." [7]

But on the other hand, there is an important passage in which Aristotle repudiates anything resembling modern situation ethics. Here he classifies some actions and feelings as absolutely evil and never even relatively desirable—feelings like malice, shamelessness, and envy, and actions like adultery, theft, and murder. These are "evil in themselves; it is not merely the excess or deficiency of them that we censure. . . . Nor do circumstances make any difference in the rightness or wrongness of them. When a man commits adultery there is no point in asking whether it is with the right woman or at the right time or in the right way, for to do anything like that is simply wrong." [8] The fact is that Aristotle's outlook is a combination of absolutism and relativism. Some things are intrinsically, absolutely wrong, while the majority of feelings and actions are to be governed by individual reason in a relativistic, perilously shifting set of relationships.

For the majority of ethical decisions, then, Aristotle advised a constant and individualized search for the Golden Mean. "It is in the nature of moral qualities," he points out, "that they can be destroyed by deficiency on the one hand and excess on the other." He illustrates this principle by referring to physical health, which can be destroyed both by too much and too little exercise, or by eating too much or too little. "Well, it is the same with temperance, courage, and the other virtues." Courage, for example, is the Golden Mean—the point of balance—between the excessive extreme of foolhardiness and the deficient extreme of cowardliness.[9] If I know myself to be cowardly, I will probably have to goad myself in the direction of the foolhardy in order to hit the balance of courage—but it is true courage which is my goal. In any situation there is no book of rules for me to follow; I am left with the responsibility of deciding what would constitute foolhardiness *for me,* cowardliness *for me,* and the correct balance-point *for me.*

There is no way to shift the responsibility, no vacation from the active use of my reason. Like the Apostle Paul, Aristotle could never sit back and say he had arrived morally, for morality is a constant struggle. Aristotle described his striving this way: "we ought, so far as in us lies, to put on immortality and to leave nothing unattempted in the effort to live in conformity with the highest thing within us." [10] To Aristotle life was a constant *becoming,* a constant process; so also with the Apostle Paul: "Brethren, I count not myself to have apprehended: but this one thing I do, forgetting those things which are behind, and reaching forth unto those things which are before, I press toward the mark for the prize of the high calling of God in Christ Jesus" (Phil. 3:13-14). And of course the concept of moderation, of "nothing in excess," is a biblical one: "Let your moderation be known unto all men" (Phil. 4:5).

Other illustrations Aristotle uses to explain his principle of the Golden Mean include temperance in pleasure, the wise use of money, proper pride, and genuine friendliness. The man who "indulges every pleasure without refraining from a single one" is guilty of the excessive extreme of incontinence or intemperance. On the other hand, the man who turns his back on every pleasure is guilty of the defective extreme of insensitivity—for his sensibilities will become blunted; he will become unimpressionable.[11] The temperate man, however, will strike a reasonable and healthful balance.

In the use of money, Aristotle counsels a mean between the excess of prodigality and the deficiency of stinginess. In the matter of honor, a man must strive for a balance-point of proper pride, which hovers perilously between the extremes of vanity and poor-spiritedness. In the matter of personal relations he must cultivate genuine friendliness as opposed to the extremes of obsequiousness or surliness.[12] Examples could, of course, be multiplied out of the experience in any human lifetime.

On the subject of self versus others, Aristotle bears interesting relationship to the ideas of Ayn Rand, who considers herself Aristotelian. Aristotle is, as usual, hard-headedly practical: "The good man is supposed never to act except on some lofty principle . . . and to neglect his own interest in order to promote that of his friend. It is a view which is not borne out by the facts." But he goes on to explain that a good man lives according to his intelligence, by reason governing himself; and "he who loves and indulges this part [the reason] is to the fullest extent a lover of himself." Such a man differs completely from the vulgar, irrational self-lover, who is subject to his own passions and thus is his own worst enemy. "Therefore it is right for the *good* man to be self-loving, because he will thereby himself be benefited by performing fine actions; and by the same process he will be helpful to others." [13]

So far Ayn Rand has very precisely followed Aristotle's ideas—precisely enough that in the subtitle of *The Virtue of Selfishness: a New Concept of Egoism,* the word *new* becomes rather amusing. But whereas Miss Rand heaps scorn on sacrificial altruism, Aristotle sees the good man as "ready to sacrifice wealth, honours, all the prizes of life in his eagerness to play a noble part." He may even lay down his life for others; but by so doing he wins for himself a crown of glory. He may lose money so that his friends may get more— but while the friends get the money, he gets the credit. "so he is assigning the greater good to himself. . . . Thus in the whole field of admirable conduct we see the good man taking a larger share of moral dignity. In this sense then it is . . . right that he should be self-loving. But in the vulgar sense no one should be so." [14]

The chief weakness of Aristotle's ethical system, like that of Ayn Rand, is that it asks of a human being more than human beings are able to perform: a total adherence to rationality. Aristotle recognizes this difficulty far more clearly than does Miss Rand: "we ought, *so far as in us lies,* to . . . live in conformity with the highest thing within us" (that is, with our reason). And of course Aristotle did not have available to him the motivation and assistance which St. Paul claimed in his struggle "toward the mark for the prize of the high calling of God in Christ Jesus." For pre-Christian Aristotle, morality was entirely a matter of responsible human effort; but for the Christian humanist, morality is a matter of responsible human effort coupled with and undergirded by the power of the Holy Spirit of God.

References for Chapter Five

[1] Henry Hazlitt, *The Foundations of Morality* (Princeton: D. Van Nostrand, 1964), p. 6.

[2] J. A. K. Thomson, ed. *The Ethics of Aristotle* (Baltimore: Penguin Books, 1955), p. 154. All subsequent quotations from the *Ethics* are drawn from this edition and are used by permission of George Allen and Unwin, Ltd., and Barnes and Noble.

[3] *Ethics*, p. 73.

[4] Brand Blanshard, *Reason and Goodness* (London: George Allen and Unwin Ltd., 1961), p. 37. Aristotle's own answer to Blanshard might well be this comment from Book Nine: "As I have so often insisted, discussions of feelings and actions admit of no more definiteness than belongs to the matter under discussion" (p. 263).

[5] *Ethics*, p. 47.

[6] *Ethics*, p. 74.

[7] *Ethics*, p. 219.

[8] *Ethics*, p. 67.

[9] *Ethics*, p. 58. Shakespeare may have been thinking of Aristotle in the *Henry IV* plays. At any rate, Hotspur clearly represents the excess of foolhardiness, Falstaff the defect of cowardliness, and the reformed Prince Hal the Golden Mean of courage.

[10] *Ethics*, p. 305.

[11] *Ethics*, p. 58, p. 68.

[12] *Ethics*, pp. 68-70.

[13] *Ethics*, pp. 273-276.

[14] *Ethics*, p. 276.

Six

Not only does man need to find a balance between too much and too little; he himself **is** a balance between two extremes: "A Nothing in comparison with the Infinite, an All in comparison with the Nothing, a mean between nothing and everything."

Chapter Six

PARADOXICAL MAN

Jumping across a span of twenty centuries, I come to another great philosophic work which stresses man's need for balance within a paradoxical reality. It is the *Pensées* of Blaise Pascal, conceived about 1660 and curiously enough, like Aristotle's *Ethics,* never put into finished form.[1] It seems right that each of these works, so concerned with growth as opposed to completion, with becoming as opposed to being— it seems right that they should be left incomplete so that one hears a man thinking out loud rather than confronting a closed and finished system.

To Pascal, paradoxes are everywhere; and because they *are* everywhere, a man must learn to encompass opposite poles of truth and establish the reality revealed by each. "When we wish to correct with advantage," says Pascal, "and to show another that he errs, we must notice from what side he views the matter, for on that side it is usually true, and admit that truth to him, but reveal to him the side on which

it is false." This is more than a seventeenth-century contribution to *How to Win Friends and Influence People;* this
is a recognition that absolute truth cannot be apprehended
absolutely by human beings, for "man naturally cannot see
everything." [2] Because he sees only relatively, man must be
willing to admit what is true about a view which radically
opposes his own.

Unlike Aristotle, Pascal knew about and trusted in the
merits of Jesus Christ, in whom he saw the central point of
balance for all men: "The knowledge of God without that
of man's misery causes pride. The knowledge of man's misery
without that of God causes despair. The knowledge of Jesus
Christ constitutes the middle course, because in Him we
find both God and our misery. Jesus Christ is a God whom
we approach without pride, and before whom we humble
ourselves without despair." [3] Here Pascal is enunciating a
paradox which many modern psychologists have failed to
grasp: there is no danger of despair in recognizing my misery
as long as I can also find forgiveness for it; and conversely
there is no danger of pride in approaching God as long as
I truly remember that my entree is Jesus Christ.

Pascal recognizes that a healthy state of mind is a complex
and paradoxical one in which confident joy is balanced by
awareness of limitation and capacity for evil: "A person told
me one day that on coming from confession he felt great joy
and confidence. Another told me that he remained in fear.
Whereupon I thought that these two together would make
one good man, and that each was wanting in that he had not
the feeling of the other. The same often happens in other
things." [4] The man who is simply confident and joyful will
tend to underestimate his own propensities for evil and to
gloss over his own imperfections. The man who is simply
fearful will be afraid to take action, cringing instead of con-

quering (like T. S. Eliot's character Prufrock). But the
healthy state of mind which Proverbs 1:7 describes as "the
fear of the Lord . . . the beginning of wisdom" is a combination of confidence and submission, joy and sorrow.

This combination is necessary because man himself is
poised halfway between God and the animals. He is both
"judge of all things" and "imbecile worm of the earth";
both "depositary of truth" and "a sink of uncertainty and
error"; both "the pride and [the] refuse of the universe!"
To Pascal "it clearly seems that man by grace is made like
unto God, and a partaker in His divinity, and that without
grace he is like unto the brute beasts." [5] Not only does man
need to find a balance between too much and too little; he
himself *is* a balance between two extremes: "A Nothing in
comparison with the Infinite, an All in comparison with the
Nothing, a mean between nothing and everything." [6]

Pascal was excruciatingly aware of the gnawing of doubt.
In nature he saw "nothing which is not matter of doubt and
concern." If he could see nothing which revealed a God, he
would peacefully become an atheist; if he clearly saw everywhere the hand of the Creator, he would peacefully believe.
But he saw neither. Here again man is confronted by a
paradoxical and perplexing reality: "seeing too much to
deny and too little to be sure, I am in a state to be pitied." [7]
He wishes that nature would either testify *unequivocally*
of God or remain silent altogether; yet his 923 *pensées*
demonstrate the fact that he did not let his doubts destroy
him. Rather, he let them prod him into thinking more and
more deeply about the nature of his faith. And perhaps that
very prodding is the reason why God created the universe as
He did, so that a thoughtful person is constantly confronted
with perplexing paradox. Again, Pascal has said it beauti-
fully: "If there were no obscurity, man would not be sensible

of his corruption; if there were no light, man would not hope for a remedy. Thus, it is not only fair, but advantageous to us, that God be partly hidden and partly revealed; since it is equally dangerous to man to know God without knowing his own wretchedness, and to know his own wretchedness without knowing God." [8]

Pascal, a great scientist-mathematician, was fully cognizant of the paradox of reason—that the highest knowledge is to know that you do *not* know: "The last proceeding of reason is to recognise that there is an infinity of things which are beyond it. It is but feeble if it does not see so far as to know this. But if natural things are beyond it, what will be said of supernatural?" [9] On the other hand, he also recognized that thinking is the essential dignity of man: "If the universe were to crush him, man would still be more noble than that which killed him, because he knows that he dies and the advantage that the universe has over him; the universe knows nothing of this. . . . By space the universe encompasses and swallows me up like an atom; by thought I comprehend the world." Man is only a reed, but he is "a thinking reed"; therefore his chief endeavor must be "to think well; this is the principle of morality." [10]

As for that good thinking, Pascal sounds very like Aristotle in his emphasis on the balance between extremes: "We do not sustain ourselves in virtue by our own strength, but by the balancing of two opposed vices, just as we remain upright amidst two contrary gales. Remove one of the vices, and we fall into the other." [11] How like the virtuous balance between the vices of foolhardiness and cowardliness, or of prodigality and stinginess!

In the reading of Scripture, as in every other area of life, Pascal recognized the importance of clear thinking and wise juxtaposition of polarities of truth: "We can only describe a good character by reconciling all contrary qualities, and it is not enough to keep up a series of harmonious qualities, without reconciling contradictory ones. To understand the meaning of an author, we must make all the contrary passages agree.

"Thus, to understand Scripture, we must have a meaning in which all the contrary passages are reconciled. It is not enough to have one which suits many concurring passages; but it is necessary to have one which reconciles even contradictory passages." [12]

This constitutes an enormous challenge to me and to twentieth-century Christians in general. Not only must I consider my behavior in the context of total Scripture and total human experience, but I am *obligated* to confront and examine views which totally oppose what I want to believe. *Obligated* to examine Scriptures at the opposite pole from the passage which I favor. *Obligated* because only in that way can I hope to come to an honest understanding of the Author's meaning. If I fear to confront scriptural paradoxes, my fear reveals my lack of faith that the Book is meaningful —I would then have to admit either that God was *not* the author, or that His thought was muddled. For, as Pascal says, "Every author has a meaning in which all the contradictory passages agree, or he has no meaning at all. We cannot affirm the latter of Scripture and the prophets; they undoubtedly are full of good sense. We must then seek for a meaning which reconciles all discrepancies." [13]

Pascal sheds a troubling light on the modern situation ethics debate, although of course he never heard of it. So keen is his awareness of paradoxical facets of truth that he knows any law can be deemed worthless from one standpoint or another. The people in general, he says, "obey laws, but they are liable to revolt when these are proved to be valueless; and *this can be shown of all, looked at from a certain aspect"* (italics mine). Therefore Pascal concludes that "it is dangerous to tell the people that the laws are unjust; for they obey them only because they think them just." [14]

Pascal's insight places a heavy responsibility on any teacher of situation ethics. He dare not assume that the members of his audience are mature, responsible Christians; for many of them are unstable and shallow in the extreme. They obey laws out of habit, because it is the thing to do; and any teaching to the contrary will not be received with thoughtful deliberation and keen responsibility, but as a *carte blanche* for violence. This is one of the reasons that I think Joseph Fletcher wrong in denying the guilt of breaking established laws or rules, even when the goal is legitimately the maintenance of a higher law. Only the man who is willing to shoulder guilt, willing to incur deep and grievous responsibility, willing to pay the price—only he is mature enough to act upon private inspiration. Like Samson, such a man lives dangerously.

What then is a teacher or a preacher supposed to do? Must he suppress the undeniable "situation ethic" aspect of the New Testament and stress only the absolutistic aspect, in order to protect his less mature listeners from taking license to sin? Here too a person will have to seek his own balance, striving to teach "all the counsel of God" (Acts 20:27) while at the same time setting that desire within the context of human experience (man's tendency to become violent and anarchic when any of the laws are questioned). For me, the point is this: I must teach with care, thoroughly, and must stress and restress the enormous responsibility incurred by laying claim to an inspiration above the law. I cannot take these things lightly, nor can I teach them lightly. But to ignore them would be to ignore passage after passage of Scripture—and I cannot and must not do that, either.

On the subject of self versus others, Pascal is typically paradoxical. In the first place, Pascal believes that "if there is a God, we must love Him only, and not the creatures of a day." Furthermore, he goes so far as to say that "we must love God only and hate self only." On the face of them, these statements sound like the worst kind of fanaticism, repugnant to a Christian humanist who values human relationships as the chief means of expressing love for God. But Pascal does paradoxically recognize that in loving God a person most truly loves both himself and others: "The true and only virtue . . . is to hate self (for we are hateful on account of lust), and to seek a truly lovable being to love. But as we cannot love what is outside ourselves [note the psychological realism], we must love a being who is in us, and is not ourselves; and that is true of each and all men. Now, only the Universal Being is such. The kingdom of God is within us; the universal good is within us, is ourselves —and not ourselves." [15]

Ourselves—and not ourselves. Paradoxical, certainly. But rightly so. To love a God who is totally *ourselves* would be to intensify all the selfishness which is already present in our fallen natures. To love a God who is totally *not ourselves* would be to spurn this life and our own potential. But instead we are told of "Christ in you, the hope of glory" (Col. 1:27): ourselves—and not ourselves.

Pascal's paradoxical insight is not so different from that of the contemporary Christian apologist H. D. Lewis: "When we find religion most certainly true to itself, the emphasis is not on the magisterial voice of a moral censor outside us but on the Kingdom of Heaven within." To Lewis as to Pascal, there is no vast dichotomy between God's power and Christian effort; we receive "illumination of mind and heart through the influence of a long-suffering and seeking God who deals with us as persons and deepens our understanding of his will for us in the refinement and deepening of our own moral understanding." [16]

Ourselves—and not ourselves.

References for Chapter Six

[1] "We must regard the *Pensées* as merely the first notes for a work which he left far from completion": T. S. Eliot, "Introduction," *Pascal's Pensées*, transl. W. F. Trotter (New York: E. P. Dutton, 1958), p. xii, Dutton Paperback Edition. All subsequent quotations from the *Pensées* are from this edition, and are used by permission of E. P. Dutton & Co., Inc.

[2] *Pensées*, No. 9, p. 4.

[3] *Pensées*, Nos. 526, 527, p. 143.

[4] *Pensées*, No. 529, p. 143.

[5] *Pensées*, No. 434, pp. 121-122.

[6] *Pensées*, No. 72, p. 17.

[7] *Pensées*, No. 229, p. 64.

[8] *Pensées*, No. 585, p. 162.

[9] *Pensées*, No. 267, p. 77.

[10] *Pensées*, Nos. 347, 348, p. 97.

[11] *Pensées*, No. 359, p. 99.

[12] *Pensées*, No. 683, p. 193.

[13] *Ibid.* The context of Pascal's hermeneutical remarks in his discussion of typology ("All that tends not to charity is figurative. The sole aim of the Scripture is charity"). Pascal thus underrates the historical aspect of the Bible but is clear concerning the spiritual level of meaning.

[14] *Pensées*, Nos. 325, 326, p. 91.

[15] *Pensées*, Nos. 479, 476, 485, pp. 132-135 passim.

[16] H. D. Lewis, "The Voice of Conscience and the Voice of God," in *Christian Ethics and Contemporary Philosophy*, ed. Ian T. Ramsey (London: SCM Press Ltd., 1966), p. 179.

Seven

To all people I owe justice, obeying rules to which I dare not make myself the exception. But with my inner circle of friends I rise beyond rules to the freedom of genuine commitment, where the only requirements are those of my personal integrity.

Chapter Seven

THE SOCIAL BALANCE

I have observed the concept of balance in two classics: one the work of a pre-Christian philosopher and one the work of a seventeenth-century Christian mathematician-philosopher. But I am a creature of the twentieth century, and I must turn to my own era. I have again selected two works, one by a man who makes no claim to Christianity and the other by an openly Christian artist. These are not works of philosophy, however, but of art—a play and a novel.

Edward Albee recently won the Pulitzer Prize for a play called *A Delicate Balance*. It is the essence of contemporaneous living, for Albee describes the entire setting in just twelve words: "The living room of a large and well-appointed suburban house. Now." The play begins and ends with Agnes, "a handsome woman in her late 50's," discussing with her husband Tobias the delicate balance between sanity and insanity, reason and unreason, order and disorder. At the beginning she is probing the possibility of going mad herself: "I might very easily—as they say—lose my mind one day, . . . I'm not that sort; . . . [but] it is not beyond . . . happening . . . becoming a stranger in the world, quite . . . uninvolved, for I never see it as violent, only a drifting." [1] At the end of the play she is pitying poor Edna and Harry because they have obviously yielded to the forces of unreason by becoming afraid to stay alone in their own house: "I wonder if that's why we sleep at night, because the darkness still . . . frightens us? They say we sleep to let the demons out—to let the mind go raving mad, our dreams and nightmares all our logic gone awry, the dark side of our reason. And when the daylight comes again . . . comes order with it." [2]

Order! The very word is ironic in the home of Tobias and Agnes. With them lives Agnes' unmarried sister Claire, a drunkard who insists she is not an alcoholic because alcoholics can't help themselves and she can, but won't. After attending several meetings of Alcoholics Anonymous, she comments, "They were sick, and I was merely . . . wilful." Also with Agnes and Tobias is their thirty-six-year-old daughter Julia, home after the break-up of her fourth marriage. Julia goes into hysterics when she discovers that her room is being occupied by Edna and Harry, the "best friends" of her parents, who had suddenly become mortally afraid of nothing in particular and had turned to the people they felt would be most willing to offer them a haven. In such a melee it is ironic to speak of order.

But that isn't the only irony of the play. If one accepts Agnes' concept of madness as "becoming a stranger in . . . the world, quite . . . uninvolved . . . only a drifting," then everyone in the play is mad. Agnes admits at the play's end that madness may have overtaken her without her knowledge: "I will, one day . . . lose my mind—but when? Never,

I begin to think, as the years go by, or that I'll not *know* if it happens, or maybe even *has.*" It has. She is uninvolved and drifting; so is Tobias; and so are Claire, Julia, Edna, and Harry.

Obviously Albee is saying something about modern society. In his own way he is saying what Robert Burton has been telling the world since the seventeenth century: "In whom doth not passion, anger, envy, discontent, fear, and sorrow reign? Who labours not of this disease? [i.e., melancholy, or madness] . . . Most men are mad." [3] But Albee concentrates on the kind of madness peculiarly intense in the twentieth century: loveless lack of involvement, with its corresponding horror of emptiness.

Agnes and Tobias are uninvolved even with each other and with their own daughter. They have not slept in the same room for a long time, and Tobias has cheated on Agnes just as Harry has cheated on Edna. They are not divorced and they are not legally separated; but as Agnes admits, life has separated them by "the gradual . . . demise of intensity, the private preoccupations, the substitutions." [4] Each of them tries to shift the burden of responsible action onto the other. Concerning the decision of whether to permit Edna and Harry to live with them in the face of Julia's hysterical desire to get her own room back, Agnes urges Tobias to take full responsibility: "We [women] follow. We let our . . . men decide the moral issues." To which Tobias replies angrily, "Never! You've never done that in your life!" [5]

Agnes and Tobias have never once attempted to help their poor maladjusted Julia make a success of one of her marriages. Tobias weakly wonders whether he should talk to Doug, the fourth husband, but he has never tried to salvage the earlier marriages with Tom, or Charlie, or Phil (whose name Agnes cannot even remember until Claire helps her out) .[6]

Much-married Julia is a selfish woman, certainly, but in her moment of need she merits real compassion. She screams "Mother? Father! Help me! !" But they do not help her; they never have. Agnes "hasn't the time" to go upstairs and tend to her hysterical daughter. When Tobias asks her to do so, she replies, "I haven't time for the four-hour talk, the soothing recapitulation. You don't go through it, my love: the history. . . . At midnight, maybe . . . when you're all in your beds, safely sleeping. Then I will comfort our Julia, and lose myself once more." *Lose myself:* is Albee consciously echoing Matthew 10:39—"He that findeth his life shall lose it: and he that loseth his life for my sake shall find it"? If so, he thus underscores what all the rest of the play implies: that by refusing to lose themselves in real commitment to the welfare of others, the characters are failing to find a meaningful life.[7]

Claire's acid comment on Agnes' attitude is only too accurate: "I tell ya, there are so many martyrdoms here." As a matter of fact, Claire is far and away the most attractive character in the play, because although she is often selfish and cynical she is at least as hard on herself as she is on other people. Disgusted with her sister's martyr-complex, Claire reminds everyone that "if you interviewed a camel, he'd admit he loved his load";[8] and she sticks by that philosophy, refusing to make excuses for her addiction to alcohol. But in fact she is wrong to deny herself the excuse of sickness, for she *is* sick—sick with a hunger for love. She reveals this as she describes drunkenness to Tobias: "You hate with the same green stinking sickness you feel your bowels have turned into . . . yourself, and *everybody*. Hate, and, oh, God! ! you want love, l-o-v-e, so badly—comfort and snuggling is what you really mean, of course—but you hate, and you notice—with a sort of detachment that amuses you, you think—that you're more like an animal every day. . . ." [9]

For all her drinking and cavorting, Claire emerges as the clearest-eyed, most loving person in the play (although that really isn't very loving at all). When the chips are down, she is willing to lie in order to spare Agnes the painful knowledge of Tobias' infidelity.[10] And her cutting comments are refreshing as compared to everyone else's self-justification. Ironically, although Agnes considers herself the fulcrum of the household, drunken Claire is more nearly the point of whatever balance there is. At least she alone is fully aware that sentimentalized love is not the answer to their problems: "You love Agnes and Agnes loves Julia and Julia loves me and I love you. We all love each other; yes we do. We love each other. . . . Yes, to the depths of our self-pity and our greed." [11]

If Tobias and Agnes are uninvolved with each other, it is hardly a surprise to discover that they are uninvolved with the people whom they call their best friends. Early in the play Claire asks Tobias whether he would give his friend Harry the shirt off his back. He supposes that he would. But he later discovers that he is not really willing to give Harry and Edna a room in his house, and he is horrified to discover how little he *likes* Harry, to say nothing of Edna. He will not force them out of his house because he has put forty years into the friendship, and he refuses to face the blank emptiness of openly admitting that all that time amounts to no relationship at all. Agnes is willing to rationalize her desire to get rid of Harry and Edna by claiming that what she and Tobias will be ousting is a disease rather than Harry and Edna themselves; but Tobias will not allow himself such a rationalization. "No, Agnes," he says; "for God's sake, if . . . if that's all Harry and Edna mean to us, then . . . then what about *us?* When we talk to each other . . . what have we meant? Anything? When we touch, when we promise, and say . . . Yes, or please . . . with *ourselves?* . . . have we meant, yes, but only if . . . If there's any condition, Agnes! Then it's . . . all been empty." [12]

Exactly: empty. Fortunately for Agnes and Tobias, Harry and Edna decide to leave of their own volition. And they make their decision because the situation has forced them to be honest about their own lovelessness. As Harry admits to Tobias, "I told Edna upstairs, I said: Edna, what if they'd come to us? And she didn't say anything. And I said: Edna, if they'd come to us like this, and even though we don't have . . . Julia, and all of that, I . . . Edna, I wouldn't take them in. I wouldn't take them in, Edna; they don't . . . they don't have the right. And she said: yes, I know, they wouldn't have the right. Toby, I wouldn't let *you* stay." [13] It is all very lonely, very sad. In turn Tobias confesses to Harry, "I find my liking you has limits. . . . The fact [is] I like you well enough, but not enough . . . that best friend in the world should be something else—more—well, that's my poverty." [14]

And the poverty of the twentieth century?

Harry's relationship to Edna is as pitiful as Tobias' to Agnes. Edna pretends she wants Harry to make love with her, knowing that he will not do so, but just to make him feel good; and she succeeds. But both of them know that their marriage is emptiness. Harry admits to Tobias that he does not talk much with his wife, and that they do not even really like each other any more; and Edna wearily admits to Agnes that "It's sad to know you've gone through it all, or most of it [life] without . . . that the one body you've wrapped your arms around . . . the only skin you've ever known . . . is your own—and that it's dry . . . and not warm." [15]

Never has the disease of selfishness been more artistically anatomized than in *A Delicate Balance*. Never has the intrinsic, built-in penalty of selfishness, empty lovelessness, been more graphically portrayed.

What is the delicate balance to which Albee's title refers? Agnes views herself as the point of balance for the whole family because she thinks she alone is "burdened with the ability to view a situation objectively while I am in it. . . . The double position of seeing not only facts but their implications . . . the longer view as well as the shorter." (This is laughably ironic, for Agnes is totally blind to her own shortcomings as wife, mother, sister, and friend). Insisting that the family observe the social amenities, she announces, "There is a balance to be maintained, after all, though the rest of you teeter, unconcerned, or uncaring, *assuming* you're on level ground . . . by divine right, I gather, though that is hardly so." [16]

The balance Agnes speaks of is, I think, the balance to which the title refers. If the whole human race is so hideously selfish that we participate in human relationships only in order to mask from ourselves the horror of emptiness, then it is essential that we preserve the delicate balance of the social amenities. I must not test any relationship to such an extent that I tip the scales and thus rip away the comfortable mask. I must play the game by never asking of anyone more than I have the right to expect. The penalty of losing my social balance is a high one: Edna and Agnes will never again be really comfortable together, nor will Harry and Tobias.

Other types of balance are referred to in the play: the delicate line between sanity and insanity, the day and night sides of the brain; the delicate line between acceptable social drinking and drinking too much; the delicate balance between doing too much for one's child and doing too little, between overprotection and carelessness; the delicate balance between hope and routine resignation; the equilibrium of maintaining individuality in a marriage without losing the intensity of union; the fine line between genuine individualism and wayward eccentricity; and the delicate balance required to maintain one's accepted picture of the world, to preserve one's comfortable categories intact ("Just think, Tobias, what would happen if the patterns changed; you wouldn't know where you stood, and the world would be full of strangers; that would never do").[17] But each of these is subsumed under the major need for tactful equilibrium, for the social sense which tells a person when he has taxed to the limit his right to another person's assistance or interest. Even a daughter has very little right to make claims on her parents after her *fourth* marriage—or does she?

Edward Albee is diagnosing the ills of twentieth-century man; he is not prescribing a cure. But his diagnosis is so keen that the way of hope is suggested, hinted at. When Eric Berne wrote his best-selling *Games People Play,* he was not encouraging people to substitute games for genuine I-Thou relationships. If it were not tragic it would be laughable that some people have used Berne's analysis of games as patterns to try in their own human relationships. For Dr. Berne makes clear in his final pages that his major reason for describing games was to make people aware of them so that they could rise above them into meaningful confrontations, where masks would be set aside. A person who has experienced reality could not deliberately utilize a game without committing that sin of all sins, the wilful manipulation of other human beings.

By the same token, Edward Albee is not *applauding* what he portrays in *A Delicate Balance;* he is describing or anatomizing an ill which it is not the artist's job to cure, but only to delineate accurately.

When Aristotle and Pascal wrote of balance, as philosophers they were projecting ideal human behavior. When Albee writes of balance, he is describing the way things are, shoddy as they may be. (Thoreau pointed out that "the mass of men lead lives of quiet desperation.")

I look at Albee's play from the standpoint of a Christian humanist. I feel grateful for the vitality of his portrait, and at the same time I feel deeply uneasy—uneasy because I can recognize in myself areas of uninvolvement which should have no place in the life of a Christian. After all, Christ was totally involved, and He bore upon His shoulders the sins of the world.

On the other hand, I am not Christ. He was both God and man, while I am only a human being, although one who claims redemption. It is impossible for me to be totally involved with all the human beings I meet, and with all the suffering of the world. Like Harvey Cox in *The Secular City,* I feel somewhat relieved by the anonymity which the mobility of modern life permits. Does that make me as loveless and empty as Agnes and Tobias, Harry and Edna? Hardly: for it is the essence of Albee's play that these people are loveless *in the closest relationships of their lives.* Agnes and Tobias maintain a legalistic justice-situation with everyone else in their immediate circle; their daughter has her rights, the best friends have theirs. This is the type of relationship which I am forced to have with my grocer, my students, most of my colleagues, and my acquaintances; but it is tragic indeed when people have lived their lives with no inner circle of genuine intimacy, so that they must eventually face the fact which Edna articulates: "the one body you've wrapped your arms around . . . the only skin you've ever known . . . is your own."

I must labor the point of a necessary distinction between the inner circle of intimate relationships and the outer one of justice-relationships, because there is a lot of talk today about total involvement. Many young people have kidded themselves that they are actually one of the totally involved, and have grandly passed judgment on the older generation for being less than totally involved. I remember one such young man—a fine-looking black college-age follower of Malcolm X. One day while we were discussing W. H. Auden's poem "Musée des Beaux Arts," this young man took issue with Auden's idea that suffering takes place alone—that the rest of the world inevitably and necessarily goes on its way while Icarus plunges to his death in the sea. I could tell by the look on his face that he really felt he was bearing the sufferings of all his black brothers in his heart at all times, and was scorning my callousness. So I asked him a question: "Are you ever happy?" "Yes, very happy," he replied. I said no more; I just waited for the truth to break. And it did, at least for the moment.

If I were totally involved with everyone in the world, I would never have a single happy moment, for there is never a moment which is not somebody's moment of anguish. *Total* involvement is impossible for less than deity; but involvement rightly should become greater as the relationship becomes closer. The tragedy of Albee's characters is that they have no genuine intimacy with any skin but their own.

No book of rules such as I follow in my business or professional dealings could or should apply to a close personal relationship. There I think not of what my friends have a

right to require of me, but of how I can promote their best
interests. Poor Tobias screams at Harry, "I DON'T WANT
YOU HERE! . . . BUT BY CHRIST YOU'RE GOING TO STAY HERE!
YOU'VE GOT THE RIGHT! THE RIGHT! DO YOU KNOW THE WORD?
THE RIGHT!"[18] Tobias is ready to do his duty by Harry and
Edna, hating it the whole time. He is relieved of that duty
only because Harry and Edna are honest enough to declare
their emptiness and admit they wouldn't do their duty by
him.

But surely personal commitments rise above mere duty!
"In all close human relationships there should be a flexibility
in our attitude to rules characteristic of the expert artist,
craftsman, or games player."[19] To all people I owe justice,
obeying rules to which I dare not make myself the exception.
But with my inner circle of friends I rise beyond rules to the
freedom of genuine commitment, where the only requirements are those of my personal integrity. And the more I
can widen that inner circle, of course, the richer I become.

None of this is intended to deny the importance of a
world-vision or of a universal concern for the state of mankind. I am talking in practical terms about everyday relationships. But it is wise to be aware of the paradoxical fact that
one must be ready to oppose father or mother, son or
daughter, wife or husband for the sake of Christ (Matt.
10:37).

For a Christian, certainly, there is one ultimate relationship which adds new meaning to all the rest. Helen Oppenheimer expresses it this way: "To be made God's children
by adoption and grace can be understood as a change of
status capable of transforming one's elementary moral categories." Through that transformation a human being can
begin to share in God's love for the whole world, so that
his circle of involvement is widened from *eros* and *philia*

to *agapé,* for "the love of God is shed abroad in our hearts by the Holy Ghost which is given unto us" (Rom. 5:5). But I must reserve for God alone "the *degree* of personal commitment . . . [called] worship." God alone deserves that highest degree of commitment, because He is "Transcendent Person." [20]

References for Chapter Seven

[1] Edward Albee, *A Delicate Balance* (New York: Pocket Books, 1966), p. 13.

[2] Albee, p. 175.

[3] Robert Burton, *The Anatomy of Melancholy,* Volume I (New York: E. P. Dutton, 1932), p. 40.

[4] Albee, p. 90.

[5] Albee, p. 138.

[6] Albee, p. 40.

[7] Albee, pp. 105, 116-117. In 1965 in New York City, Albee was asked about the Christian imagery and implication in his work. He disclaimed personal belief in Christianity and surmised that the images must arise "from some sort of racial memory."

[8] Albee, p. 117.

[9] Albee, p. 32.

[10] Albee, p. 109. Although Claire denies knowledge of Tobias' sex life, she knows all about his summertime infidelity: see p. 29.

[11] Albee, pp. 46-47.

[12] Albee, p. 156.

[13] Albee, pp. 163-164.

[14] Albee, p. 166.

[15] Albee, p. 169.

[16] Albee, p. 89.

[17] Albee, p. 150.

[18] Albee, p. 167.

[19] P. H. Newell-Smith, "Morality: Religious and Secular," in *Christian Ethics and Contemporary Philosophy,* ed. Ian T. Ramsey (London: SCM Press Ltd., 1966), p. 111.

[20] Helen Oppenheimer, "Moral Choice and Divine Authority," in *Christian Ethics and Contemporary Philosophy,* pp. 231-233.

Eight

The Tiger-Christ who roared furious imprecations at the Pharisees and overturned the money-tables in the Temple was the same Christ who forgave those who were nailing Him to the cross and who instructed His disciples to forgive and even love their enemies. Christ the Tiger is also Christ the Lamb.

Chapter Eight

THE TIGER AND THE LAMB

Flannery O'Connor's *The Violent Bear It Away* is as troubling a novel as a person might care to read. Miss O'Connor, who died at the age of thirty-nine, was a devout Roman Catholic. In the Spring of 1957 she told an audience at Notre Dame University that "to recognize the grotesque, you have to have some notion of what is not grotesque and why. . . . Southern culture has fostered a type of imagination that has been influenced by Christianity of a not too unorthodox kind and by a strong devotion to the Bible, which has kept our minds attached to the concrete and living symbol. . . . The Catholic sacramental view of life is one that maintains and supports at every turn the vision that the story teller must have if he is going to write fiction of any depth." [1]

Anyone who knows Miss O'Connor's work knows that the vision of which she spoke was far from comfortable. In *Everything That Rises Must Converge* she has written a group of stories which are so devastating to human pride that they leave a sensitive reader floored, flattened, prostrate —with no hope but the hope of the Cross. And that, I'm sure, was her intention.

Miss O'Connor drew the title of her 1960 novel, *The Violent Bear It Away,* from Matthew 11:12, which she quotes in full: "From the days of John the Baptist until now, the kingdom of heaven suffereth violence, and the violent bear it away." The King James Version of the final phrase is perhaps clearer: "the violent take it by force." The passage is also clarified by comparison with Luke 16:16: "The law and the prophets were until John: since that time the kingdom of God is preached, and every man presseth into it." The meaning seems to be this: as Matthew 23:13 indicates, the scribes and Pharisees were doing their best to keep men from entering the kingdom of heaven through belief in Christ. Therefore only the violently energetic—those who could press or force their way through all opposition—would be able to attain a place in the kingdom. For Miss O'Connor, contemporary opposition to the kingdom comes from modern counterparts to the hypocritical scribes and Pharisees: from psychologists and social workers and intellectuals like Rayber. And only the violent, like Mason Tarwater and his nephew Francis Marion Tarwater, are able to force entry into the kingdom of heaven.

At any rate, that is the reading which Robert Drake gives the novel.[2] And behind his reading lies the approval of Flannery O'Connor herself, for she called his long *Modern Age* review of *The Violent Bear It Away* the best review the novel had received, and at other times made various comments which support this interpretation. Drake emphasizes that for Miss O'Connor, Christ is the destroyer of all balance, an offense and a stumbling block, a "bleeding stinking mad" grotesque figure. Religion is not for moderates. Moderation is rational, and rationalists are opposed to the kingdom. Drake fully agrees with what he considers Miss O'Connor's position: "In the Christian view, Christ is the great Misfit, the Great Displaced Person, resented and scorned by the righteous and the self-justified but Himself a Great Displacer of those very same righteous: He *does* upset the balance in their lives." [3]

From one point of view this concept of Christ is absolutely correct. But it stresses one pole of scriptural truth to the exclusion of its opposite. The Tiger-Christ who roared furious imprecations at the Pharisees and overturned the money-tables in the Temple was the same Christ who forgave those who were nailing Him to the cross and who instructed His disciples to forgive and even love their enemies. Christ the Tiger is also Christ the Lamb. And although Matthew 11:12 says that the kingdom of heaven must be taken by force, another passage in Matthew (18:3) tells a different story: "Except ye be converted, and become as little children, ye shall not enter into the kingdom of heaven"—from the context, a reference to the humble simplicity of children. It is certain that the primary characteristics of the kingdom-dwellers do not include arrogance and violence: "For the kingdom of God is not meat and drink; but righteousness, and peace, and joy in the Holy Ghost. . . . Let us therefore follow after the things which make for peace, and things wherewith one may edify another" (Rom. 14:17, 19). Nothing could be farther from a description of old and young Tarwater, who apparently represent Flannery O'Connor's concept of the redeemed.

The Violent Bear It Away is the story of young Francis Marion Tarwater, caught between the lures of the two uncles who also represent conflicting elements in his own soul. Rayber, the schoolteacher-uncle, represents naturalistic existentialism, and is seconded within young Tarwater by the voice of the stranger who later calls himself the friend (a voice which Rainulf A. Stelzmann, Robert Fitzgerald, Drake, and O'Connor herself equate with the Devil). Mason Tarwater, the prophet-uncle who kidnapped young Tarwater in order to bring him up as a Christian and a prophet, is a rabid fundamentalist who plans to eat the Lord's multiplied loaves and fishes for all eternity. When Rayber tries to assert his guardianship over young Tarwater, Mason shoots him in the leg and ear; and at the urging of the woman social worker who had accompanied him, Rayber does not return a second time for his charge. Instead he marries the social worker and produces an idiot son named Bishop.

Rayber is convinced that Old Tarwater's religious views have an interesting psychological basis. Once he had written an article for a learned journal about Old Tarwater, an act for which the old man had no forgiveness. In it Rayber had theorized, "His fixation of being called by the Lord had its origin in insecurity. He needed the assurance of a call, and so he called himself." The self-dramatizing words in which the old man rages against this view do more to support than refute it: "I, Mason Tarwater, called myself! Called myself to be beaten and tied up. Called myself to be spit on and snickered at. Called myself to be struck down in my pride. Called myself to be torn by the Lord's eye." [4]

Old Tarwater is perfectly willing to cheat Rayber out of his rightful property, except that he can find no lawyer who knows how to do it. And he feels no reluctance about shooting Rayber—only satisfaction. Yet serving the Lord is entirely a matter of hardship to the old man, for he believes that even the mercy of the Lord is a consuming fire; when it all gets too much for him he feels no guilt at getting drunk.

He even runs his own still. And he feels no guilt about working violence on a child's imagination, shaking the boy by the suspenders, hissing and groaning at the thought of the Lord's mercy, and threatening the boy with the Lord's lion should he allow Mason to be burnt rather than buried.

Rayber, on the other hand, has struggled all his life to get over the four days in his youth when Mason had kidnapped and converted him. "You're too blind to see what you did to me," he later tells Mason. "A child can't defend himself. Children are cursed with believing. You pushed me out of the real world and I stayed out of it until I didn't know which was which. You infected me with your idiot hopes, your foolish violence." [5]

When Rayber sees young Tarwater at his door after Mason's death, his eyes light up with pleasure: "It's not too late for me to make a man of you!" But the boy's face darkens at this: he has sense enough to know that he is in danger of becoming clay for someone else's molding. Old Tarwater had tried to mold him one way, and now the schoolteacher wants to mold him another. And the boy's instincts are right. With all the best motives in the world, Rayber is gazing "through the actual insignificant boy before him to an image of him that he held fully developed in his own mind." [6] Young Tarwater has simply jumped from the frying pan into the fire.

Rayber becomes frustrated as his plans for the boy are balked by "the brand of independence the old man had wrought—not a constructive independence but one that was irrational, backwoods, and ignorant." [7] But he checks his impatience because "Although Tarwater claimed to believe nothing the old man had taught him, Rayber could see clearly that there was still a backdrag of belief and fear in him keeping his responses checked." [8]

[127

In Search of Balance

Young Tarwater finally recognizes his destiny as a prophet through his relationship to Rayber's idiot son, significantly named Bishop. (Like Nathaniel Hawthorne whom she admired, Flannery O'Connor was not afraid of allegory). The moment of confrontation with Bishop is the moment of revelation for young Tarwater: "He did not look into the eyes of any fiery beast or see a burning bush. He only knew, with a certainty sunk in despair, that he was expected to baptize the child he saw and begin the life his great-uncle had prepared him for." He sees himself "trudging into the distance in the bleeding stinking mad shadow of Jesus, until at last he received his reward, a broken fish, a multiplied loaf." [9]

Tarwater fights that future with everything in him. He even decides to drown Bishop as his energetic way of refusing to baptize him: "You can't just say NO. . . . You got to do NO. You got to show it. You got to show what you mean by doing it. You got to show you're not going to do one thing by doing another. You got to make an end of it. One way or another." [10] But at the very moment of Bishop's death he finds himself repeating the words of baptism.

What, exactly, constitutes "the Lord's call" to young Tarwater? There is nothing which is not easily explainable by naturalistic means: Bishop naturally causes a "revelation" because the old man had talked so incessantly about baptizing him, and the burning bush which Tarwater sees at the time he hears the call is the fire he himself set in his repudiation of the Rayber-part of his own soul. The terrible hunger he feels for the Bread of Life has both a physical and a psychological basis: he has not been able to stomach food since drowning Bishop and therefore is getting literally hungry, and he has been trained since babyhood to think in terms of Jesus as the Bread of Life. Even as he makes his final attempt to escape becoming a prophet, he is trapped within Uncle Mason's rhetoric: "The clearing was burned free of all that had ever oppressed him. No cross was there to say that this was ground that the Lord still held. What he looked out upon was the sign of a broken covenant." When he finally hears the Lord's voice, the words are clearly a combination of his great-uncle's oft-repeated words ("Go warn the children of God, saith the Lord, 'of the terrible speed of justice.' Who will be left . . . when the Lord's mercy strikes?") [11]

When Tarwater is commanded to "Go warn the children of God of the terrible speed of mercy," [12] is the charge from God, or from Mason Tarwater? And when the boy anoints his forehead with dirt from his great-uncle's grave, who can resist seeing this as a symbol of his psychic submission to all he had been taught? And are we to believe that there is nothing of ego in young Tarwater's impression that he is confronted by "the fire that had encircled Daniel, that had raised Elijah from the earth, that had spoken to Moses"? Exactly as he had dreamed it would be! [13]

I must confess that *The Violent Bear It Away* evokes mixed emotions in me. As a Christian humanist, I am delighted with Miss O'Connor's dazzling technique, her sheer style. I could pick out a hundred examples, but take just this one, a description of young Tarwater as he takes his first drink of hard liquor: "A burning arm slid down Tarwater's throat as if the devil were already reaching inside him to finger his soul." [14] For economy and vivid energy, you can't do much better than that!

But at the same time that I am delighted with her style, I am appalled by her concept of Christ, Christianity, and Christians. Her Christ is wild and furious, her Christianity is violent and irrational, her Christians are freaks. I cannot imagine anyone's being attracted to Christ by Miss O'Connor's portrayal here; yet I have already admitted that some of her stories strike at the roots of pride until in desperation one thinks of redemption as the only hope. For that, of course, I am grateful.

But looking at one of Miss O'Connor's Christians—Old Tarwater, for example—I get the shudders. Tarwater proclaims God's will for himself and others as he kidnaps youngsters, shoots his nephew Rayber, and attempts to cheat him out of his lawful property. If we are not to read Miss O'Connor as mocking the Southern fundamentalist, and we definitely are not, then I must apply to Mason Tarwater the words of Graeme de Graaf: "If there is one thing worse than a straight-cut moral blunder, it is a moral blunder for which the agent claims that God is in it with him." [15] And Ian T. Ramsey as well: "The believer must remember that in talking of God's will or God's command he is talking about God and not about man. . . . Meanwhile we must regretfully admit that . . . the unbeliever . . . gets all the fuel he needs . . . from believers who are careless enough in their expressions not only to neglect the logic of their assertions, but on that account to talk sometimes in a way that is near-blasphemous." [16]

Don't misunderstand me: I thank God for the superb artistry of His servant, Flannery O'Connor. But I grieve that in *The Violent Bear It Away* and in certain other stories she has emphasized the New Testament strain of violence (which is certainly there) to the exclusion of the New Testament strain of gentleness—poles of truth which must certainly be studied in balance with each other. And I grieve that the choice which confronts the reader of *The Violent Bear It Away* is either insane and immoral Christianity or decent, moral, but unbelieving humanism.

I think I understand why she did it this way—to dramatize the offense of the cross and the fact that not many wise are called. And if the world is deaf, you shout, you exaggerate, you utilize the grotesque! I also think she was trying to crush the ego of those Christians who think that their own good works just *might* have something to do with their being chosen of God; no one could imagine such a thing about mad old Tarwater or arrogant young Tarwater. But she handled that theme with greater clarity in her superb short story "Revelation," where Mrs. Turpin has a vision of the first last and the last first. She discovers that even the respectable first who have been made last in Christ's processional (including herself) wear "shocked and altered faces" because "even their virtues were being burned away." [17] On the basis of New Testament descriptions of the judgment of human works, I question the subject-matter of even this vision; but that's neither here nor there.

It may seem strange that I have chosen to conclude a book in search of balance by discussing a novel in which there seems to be no balance—only a brawling, irrational, uneducated belief on the one hand, and an idealistic, reasonable, educated unbelief on the other. Old Tarwater so impresses upon his nephew the good fortune of avoiding the contamination of school that the boy comes to consider his escape from school "the surest sign of his election." [18] Young Tarwater sees himself as the companion of Abel and Enoch, Noah and Job, Abraham and Moses, King David and Solomon, forgetting about the superior schooling some of them had received (cf. Acts 7:22: "And Moses was learned in all the wisdom of the Egyptians").

I suppose what I am trying to say is this: the Christian who could speak meaningfully to the twentieth-century would have to be one on the model of St. Paul: tough-minded, well-educated, perfectly rational, yet in love with God, submissive to God, eager to serve God and his fellow man. Neither a Rayber nor a Tarwater, but a combination of the better qualities of both.

In other words, balanced.

References for Chapter Eight

[1] Flannery O'Connor, as quoted by Robert Fitzgerald, "Introduction," *Everything That Rises Must Converge,* by Flannery O'Connor (New York: Farrar, Straus and Giroux, 1965), pp. 20-21. Copyright © 1955, 1960 by Flannery O'Connor.

[2] Robert Drake, *Flannery O'Connor: A Critical Essay.* Contemporary Writers in Christian Perspective (Grand Rapids, Michigan: Wm. B. Eerdmans, 1966), pp. 33-37. P. Albert Duhamel agrees: "In her works true vision is vouchsafed only to the violent like Tarwater and his great-uncle because they are people of feeling who come to recognize the inadequacy of the merely rationalistic." See Duhamel, "The Novelist As Prophet," in *The Added Dimension: The Art and Mind of Flannery O'Connor,* ed. Melvin J. Friedman and Lewis A. Lawson (New York: Fordham University Press, 1966). Also in support of Drake is Miss O'Connor's comment to Granville Hicks, published in *Saturday Review* (May 12, 1962): "Old Tarwater is the hero of 'The Violent Bear It Away,' and I'm right behind him 100 per cent."

[3] Drake, p. 27.

[4] Flannery O'Connor, *The Violent Bear It Away* (New York: Noonday Press, 1960), pp. 19-20.

[5] *Violent,* p. 73. Stanley Edgar Hyman sees Rayber as a "mad fanatic preaching secular salvation" (*Flannery O'Connor.* Minneapolis: University of Minnesota Press, 1966, p. 24). But "mad fanatic" hardly describes Rayber's mechanical control. More plausible is the comment by Louis D. Rubin, Jr., that Rayber and others fail to rescue Tarwater "by the reality of love." Because Rayber is afraid of emotion, he can offer the boy only a "complacent scientific rationalism" instead of the love he needs. Ultimately, the price Tarwater must pay for the attainment of [Bible Belt] faith is the denial and utter extinction of the possibility of love." See Rubin, "Flannery O'Connor and the Bible Belt," in *The Added Dimension: The Art and Mind of Flannery O'Connor,* p. 66.

[6] *Violent,* p. 90.

[7] *Violent,* p. 100.

[8] *Violent,* p. 115.

[9] *Violent,* p. 91.

[10] *Violent,* p. 157.

[11] *Violent,* pp. 237, 242. Cf. p. 60.

[12] *Violent,* p. 242.

[13] Cf. *Violent,* p. 41. But Miss O'Connor insists that "Tarwater is certainly free and meant to be; if he appears to have a compulsion to be a prophet, I can only insist that in this compulsion there is the mystery of God's will for him and that it is not a compulsion in the clinical sense." See Flannery O'Connor, "The Novelist and Free Will," *Fresco* (Winter, 1963).

[14] *Violent,* p. 45.

[15] Graeme de Graaf, "God and Morality," in *Christian Ethics and Contemporary Philosophy,* ed. Ian T. Ramsey (London: SCM Press Ltd., 1966), p. 47.

[16] Ian T. Ramsey, "Moral Judgments and God's Commands," in *Christian Ethics and Contemporary Philosophy,* p. 171.

[17] Flannery O'Connor, *Everything That Rises Must Converge,* p. 238.

[18] *Violent,* p. 17.

Postscript

It is difficult for anyone to appreciate the absolute until he has become painfully aware of the relative.

Postscript

A MISCELLANY OF BIBLICAL PARADOXES

The famous essayist Montaigne felt that "the natural condition of man is to make his way among enigmas, puzzles, antinomies, and contradictions, and to work through the paradoxes, physical, intellectual, and spiritual, that life invariably presents." Obviously, I think the same.

According to the *American College Dictionary*, a paradox is "a statement or proposition apparently self-contradictory or absurd, and yet explicable as expressing a truth." Because life is full of paradoxes, the Bible, which is a realistic book, is also full of paradoxes. I have tried to demonstrate that interpretations which fail to consider both poles of a biblical paradox are oversimplifications, too easy and too simple to accord with reality. But here are a few of them which did not turn up elsewhere in this book. You will probably be able to add some of your own.

No fact could be more paradoxical than the Trinity, as anyone knows who has tried to be honest and logical on the subject. I do not refer to people who are satisfied with metaphors such as the steam, ice, and liquid forms of water; I refer to people who have wrestled with the logic of three in one, one in three. If a person refuses to refer to mystery, he will almost invariably be branded a heretic by some type of Christian, as John Milton was for his heroic attempt in *De Doctrina Christiana.*

Or take the paradox of the incarnation: a man who is truly God, God who is truly man. Pascal points out that Arians refuse to see these truths as compatible. They will admit that Christ is man but deny that He is God; therefore, "exclusion is the cause of their heresy." [1]

And what about the nature of man? Psalm 82:6 says that men are gods, and this passage is quoted by Christ Himself in John 10:34; but Isaiah 40:6-7 says that men are grass, and this passage is quoted by St. Peter (I Pet. 1:24-25) and alluded to by St. James (1:10-11). Gods or grass? Both. Jesus explains in John 10:35 that men are gods because the Word of God has come unto them, because they have a spiritual dimension; Isaiah is stressing the ephemerality of man's life upon earth. In order to realize the value of keeping these truths in balance, you have only to talk to some of the contemporary college students who are convinced that man is *nothing but* "grass"—a purely physical mechanism. This view often has devastating effects on morality. So does the opposite view, in which men forget their mortality and assume that they know the mind of God both for themselves and others. But this godlike stance is hard to maintain, because the facts of human frailty and animality keep breaking in.

Closely related is the paradox of man's depravity. Genesis 8:21 says that "the imagination of man's heart is evil from his youth," but Proverbs 20:27 says that "the spirit of man is the candle of the Lord, searching all the inward parts of the belly," while Proverbs 8:31 says that the delights of wisdom were "with the sons of men." Many Christians have heard a great deal about the depravity of man; they have heard very little about his rational power and glory. Yet St. Luke did not disdain to say that Christ grew in favor with man as well as with God; so the fact could not have been totally .unimportant. To teach people that they are made in the image of God without stressing the effects of sin is to create false confidence and fatal delusions of grandeur. But to stress the effects of sin without recognizing the remnants of God's image in man—that man's spirit *is* created to be the candle of the Lord—is to set in motion some very serious psychological effects: scorn of human reason, self-disgust, and despair. If you call a person a thief long enough, sooner or later he will shrug his shoulders and steal; if he has the name, he might as well play the game. Tell a child that he is stupid often enough, and his grades will prove it. One has to be careful about applying labels, either to an individual or to the human race. The Bible stresses sin only to bring man to the Savior; it casts down only to raise up. And it does not deny the human beauty which is present in many unregenerate people, as witness the description of Cornelius before his conversion (Acts 10:1-2).

Which brings us to another paradox: the paradox of righteousness. Isaiah 64:6 identifies all of man's righteousness as "filthy rags"; it is in the strain of this passage that Flannery O'Connor envisions even the *virtues* of the redeemed as being purged away upon entry into the Kingdom. This is the great emphasis of fundamentalism, evangelicalism, and Reformed theology. There is constant attack on those who, "being ignorant of God's righteousness, and going about to establish their own righteousness, have not submitted themselves unto the righteousness of God. For Christ is the end of the law for righteousness to every one that believeth" (Rom. 10:3-4). These verses and others like them emphasize that men are not redeemed on the basis of their own merits, and thank God for that. ("Use every man after his desert, and who should 'scape whipping?") It is most certainly "not by works of righteousness which we have done, but according to his mercy he saved us" (Titus 3:5).

But to stress this undeniably true facet of Scripture to the exclusion of the many passages in praise of righteousness (honesty, integrity, uprightness) is to tamper dangerously with the truth, and to breed a scorn for human equity which can have very serious moral consequences. The fundamentalist who cannot be trusted in his business dealings is not as scarce as he should be; I could name names and probably so could you.

A glance through any good concordance will prove that in the Bible there is no disrespect for human righteousness *except when that righteousness is substituted for Christ's redemptive death as the basis for man's eternal salvation.* In Matthew 5:6 Christ pronounces blessing on those who "hunger and thirst after righteousness"; a few verses later He blesses those who are "persecuted for righteousness' sake." In Acts 10:35 Peter recognizes that "in every nation he that feareth him, and worketh righteousness, is accepted with him [God]." Psalm 11:7 assures us that "the righteous Lord loveth righteousness"; while Psalm 45:7 indicates that God loves righteousness and hates wickedness, a fact which is reiterated in Hebrews 1:9. There is no reason to explain all this away as meaning *only* that God loves those who are clothed in Christ's blood and therefore are made righteous. The evidence indicates that He loves righteousness itself, righteous acts themselves, just as He hates wicked acts in and of themselves. From the *ultimate* point of view, no righteousness will be sufficient to save a man, to blot out his sins, except the righteousness of the Perfect Man, Jesus Christ the Righteous; but from the *penultimate* point of view—from the temporal plane where we live our human lives—it is only right to respect and praise and emulate the human characteristics which reason, tradition, and Revelation recognize as righteous.

I labor this point because there are some very sincere Christians who think it is dangerous to praise as righteous the acts or words of any man who does not claim to be saved by faith in Christ. I think that such Christians are confusing the ultimate, absolute, divine view with the temporal, relative, human view. In the eyes of a perfect God, no human righteousness could be unflawed enough without the payment of a perfect redemption; but I am not God, and it is only decent for me to show respect for any relatively righteous act or word or person, and to lend my support to the apparently righteous causes I may encounter.

As for the ultimate judgment about a man's eternal state, I must leave that to God's mercy and justice. Because I am not a theologian, I will not attempt to discuss exactly what "faith in Christ" or "believing on Him" means. But I agree with Bonhoeffer that people had better beware of the doctrine of "cheap grace"; for "as the body without the spirit is dead, so faith without works is dead also" (James 2:26). Bonhoeffer brilliantly expresses the paradox of faith and works: "There is . . . no other means of access to the justification of my life than through *faith alone. But faith never is alone.* . . . It would be a false faith, . . . a hypocritical and self-invented faith such as can never justify, if it were not accompanied by love and hope. It would be a vain repetition of articles of faith, a dead faith, if it were not

[141

accompanied by the works of penitence and love" (italics mine).[2]

Another grievous paradox is the one concerning predestination and free will. Milton left this question to the fallen angels, who vainly debated

> Fixt Fate, Free Will, foreknowledge absolute
> And found no end, in wand'ring mazes lost.[3]

But it was only the *debating* which Milton found futile; for he knew that no person, not even an angel, could comprehend the mysterious point of precise balance between these opposite biblical truths. Because that point had not been revealed, it had to remain a mystery. So Milton's great epic upholds both truths: God *does* foreknow and predestinate, and since His knowledge is perfect He foreknows only that which is true.[4] Some passages, indeed, sound as if man has no self-determination whatsoever: "Ye have not chosen me, but I have chosen you, and ordained you, that ye should go and bring forth fruit" (John 15:16), or "No man can come to me, except the Father which hath sent me draw him" (John 6:44). Yet at the same time, man's will is free, incontrovertibly free, and his business in this world is to use that free will to make morally worthy choices and to seek Christ's redemption (see John 3:16; John 5:24; Matt. 11:28; and so forth). There can be no doubt that responsibility is laid squarely upon the shoulders of the individual: "See, I have set before thee this day life and good, and death and evil; in that I command thee this day to love the Lord thy God, to walk in his ways, and to keep his commandments and his statutes and his judgments . . . therefore choose life, that both thou and thy seed may live" (Deut. 30:15-16, 19).

Long before Milton, Geoffrey Chaucer had carefully retreated from any attempt to explain how God's determinations and man's freedom could simultaneously be operative. Some critics have been foolish enough to accuse Chaucer of irresponsibility for retreating into his stance of "I'm not a theologian, don't ask me." They have failed to realize that the essence of wisdom is to keep silence before an insoluble mystery—and also that Chaucer was possibly poking fun at those theologians who did dare to set themselves up as oracles concerning such a thorny question.

I have met Christians who have felt responsible to resolve the paradox of determinism and free will, as if this were specifically a Christian problem which it is specifically the Christian's responsibility to explain. Not so. Homer, writer of the oldest complete books in the Western world, recognized the problem very clearly. In the *Odyssey* he represents Zeus speaking to the other gods: "Lo you now, how vainly mortal men do blame the gods! For of us they say comes evil, whereas they even of themselves, through the blindness of their own hearts, have sorrows beyond that which is ordained." [5]

Note that Homer does not deny that man's sorrows *are* ordained; neither does he deny that man can partially control his own fate. What he *does* deny is that any man is justified in repudiating personal responsibility for his life. It seems to me that a Christian can do no less as he takes his stand against the currents of naturalistic and psychological determinism in today's thinking.

Still another paradox is the paradox of truth, which according to the Bible is both victor and vanquished. The Psalms are full of promises that truth will triumph: Psalm 100:5, for instance, promises that God's "truth endureth to all generations"; Psalm 117:2 asserts that "the truth of the Lord endureth forever"; and Psalm 91:4-7 promises that if God's truth is man's shield and buckler, "a thousand shall fall at thy side, and ten thousand at thy right hand, but it shall not come nigh thee." But Isaiah 59:14-15 tells a different tale: "Judgment is turned away backward, and justice standeth afar off: for truth is fallen in the street, and equity cannot enter. Yea, truth faileth; and he that departeth from evil maketh himself a prey." There are scriptural instances of the defeat of godly and righteous people and causes. Human experience, of course, abounds with them.

There is an American organization called Debate Records which stages, records, and sells phonograph records of debates on various significant topics. The letterhead of this organization carries quotations concerning truth and argumentation by twelve great writers or orators, and these quotations dramatize the paradox of truth which I am talking about. The most famous of all the quotations is the most false, unless it is read very carefully as Milton no doubt meant it in the context of *Areopagitica:* "Let truth and falsehood grapple; who ever knew truth put to the worse in a free and open encounter?" In the context of a debate, I would be the first to say that *I have:* for in debate it is often not truth which carries the day, but rather the most persuasive speaker. The quotation from Montaigne implies as much: "He who establishes his argument by noise and command, shows that his reason is weak."

But to be fully honest to the facts of debate, that record company ought to add to its letterhead the following quotation from Sir Thomas Browne's *Religio Medici:* "Every man is not a proper champion for Truth, nor fit to take up the gauntlet in the cause of Veritie. . . . A man may be in as just possession of Truth as of a City, and yet be forced to surrender; 'tis better therefore to enjoy her with peace, than to hazard her on a battle." In plain words, if you aren't equipped with a logical mind and an eloquent tongue, you will do truth and yourself more of a favor by keeping silence than by argumentation. Every man to his own gift.

The paradox of truth is easier than most to resolve, but harder than most to remember. The positive promises of God about the unassailable nature of truth and truth's champions are ultimate promises referring to the eternal state of things; while the passages concerning truth in defeat refer to the penultimate state of human life as we know it. The paradox is in fact resolved rather neatly in Psalm 73, which begins with envy at the prosperity of the wicked, reaches its turning point in the sanctuary of God when the speaker comes to understand the end of the wicked, and concludes with the realization that after all it *is* good to trust in God. Alas, we have to live through the experience of Psalm 73 all too many times before the conclusion becomes habitual.

I could go on and on digging up biblical paradoxes, but we have to stop somewhere. One more, though: the paradox of knowledge, which I touched on in connection with Pascal. St. Paul prayed that the church at Ephesus might "know the love of Christ, which passeth knowledge" (3:19). How can one know what is beyond knowing? Yet this is really the ultimate achievement of knowing—that a person is equipped to recognize what he does not know. This was the wisdom of Socrates. And to Montaigne the ultimate knowledge is that each man must learn his own foolishness: "To know oneself comes in the end to the fact that one cannot know one's self, because one has no instruments to plumb the depths of that ever-changing creature, and because, really, one has not the means to know anything at all, not even, or especially not, one's self." [6] This does not excuse a person from studying, or from acting on responsible decisions. It is the condition of humanity that a wise man must live perpetually aware of his ignorance yet perpetually responsible to the truth.

If I cannot know even myself, how much less can I know God! Yet because of biblical revelation I *can* know God, *can* "know the love of Christ, which passeth knowledge." In fact, the more I know about the love of Christ as I learn to experience that love in the conditions of everyday life, the more certain I will become that His love *does* surpass knowledge. Increasingly I will become amazed at what I know I do not know: "O the depth of the riches both of the wisdom and knowledge of God! How unsearchable are his judgments, and his ways past finding out!" (Rom. 11:33).

To conclude: irony and paradox are qualities which are highly valued by modern critics of secular literature. Irony has been defined as "a refusal of complete commitment to any simple view of experience, a sense that life is filled with contradictions and that all truths are partial, all values imperfect, to be qualified by other truths and other values." [7] Naturally, this irony is often best expressed by paradox, either overt or implied.

In a now-famous lecture "Pure and Impure Poetry" given at Princeton in 1942, Robert Penn Warren declared that a good poet must make clear that "his vision has been earned, that it can survive reference to the complexities and contradictions of experience." [8] Certainly, the vision of a good poet should not have to earn itself with any more integrity than the vision of an honest interpreter of the Bible. A preacher or teacher of the Scripture must also prove that "his vision has been earned, that it can survive reference to the complexities and contradictions of experience." He can hardly do this if he teaches only one half of a biblical paradox and ignores the existence of the other half. As Rosalie Colie says of all paradoxes, "One meaning can never outweigh the other, though weighed to eternity. The one meaning must always be taken with respect to the other." [9]

Here follows space for an enterprising reader to make his own list of biblical paradoxes, remembering that the full context of any passage must be the whole Bible and the accumulated experience of mankind.

TRUTH..........	TO BE BALANCED ...... BY	OPPOSITE ....TRUTH
	(LIST HERE COMMENTS ON HOW THE PARADOX IS RESOLVED, IF INDEED IT IS).	
"Come out from among them, and be ye separate, saith the Lord, and touch not the unclean thing" II Cor. 6:17.	*I must distinguish between essentials and nonessentials of belief, and must be careful not to cause rifts for carnal, loveless reasons—yet unafraid to cause them for basic realities.*	"And this commandment have we from him, That he who loveth God love his brother also" I John 4:21.

In Search of Balance

	TO BE BALANCED	
TRUTH.......	...... BY	......OPPOSITE TRUTH

TRUTH..........	TO BE BALANCED BY	OPPOSITE .... TRUTH

There is a frightening paradox implied in the first three verses of I Corinthians 13—frightening in that a person may do all the right things, all the things commonly associated with godliness and love, and yet be totally lacking in love, completely devoid of the spirit of Christ. "Though I speak with the tongues of men and of angels, and have not charity, I am become as sounding brass, or a tinkling cymbal"—I might have powers of total communication without having a loving spirit. "And though I have the gift of prophecy, and understand all mysteries, and all knowledge; and though I have all faith, so that I could remove mountains, and have not charity, I am nothing"—I might have total insight into God's truth and total access to His power (imagine!) without having a loving spirit. "And though I bestow all my goods

[149

to feed the poor, and though I give my body to be burned, and have not charity, it profiteth me nothing." John 15:13 says that there is no greater love than the love in which a man lays down his life for his friend; yet I Corinthians 13:3 says that it is possible for a person to go even beyond this personal sacrifice in the altruism of impoverishing himself and even of giving his body to be burned for the good of others *without being loving at all!*

Human motives cannot, then, be judged by external standards. Like St. Paul, twentieth-century Christians cannot *ultimately* judge even their own actions, much less someone else's. Paradoxically, an awareness of the limitations and subjectivity of my human condition throws me into total dependence upon the ultimate absolute judgment and mercy of God. It is difficult for anyone to appreciate the absolute until he has become painfully aware of the relative.

As I exercise my privilege of interpreting Scripture, it is essential that I open my mind to both poles of paradoxical truths, teaching them and living in awareness of them, so that my vision may "survive reference to the complexities and contradictions of experience."

This commits me, I know, to a continual search for a continually shifting balance.

And search I will.

References for Postscript

[1] *Pensées*, No. 861, p. 258.

[2] *Ethics*, (New York: The Macmillan Company, 1955), pp. 121-122.

[3] *Paradise Lost*, II. 559-60.

[4] See Acts 2:23; Rom. 8:29-30; Eph. 1:4-5, 11; and so forth.

[5] *The Odyssey of Homer*, trans. S. H. Butcher and A. Lang (New York: Modern Library, 1950), p. 2.

[6] See Rosalie Colie, *Paradoxia Epidemica* (Princeton: Princeton University Press, 1966), p. 392.

[7] M. K. Danziger and W. S. Johnson, *An Introduction to Literary Criticism* (Boston: D. C. Heath & Co., 1961), p. 178.

[8] See David Daiches, *Critical Approaches to Literature* (New York: Prentice-Hall, 1956), p. 161.

[9] *Paradoxia Epidemica*, p. 6.